Comments on other *Amazing Stories* from readers & reviewers

"*Tightly written volumes filled with lots of wit and humour about famous and infamous Canadians.*"
Eric Shackleton, *The Globe and Mail*

"*The heightened sense of drama and intrigue, combined with a good dose of human interest is what sets* Amazing Stories *apart.*"
Pamela Klaffke, *Calgary Herald*

"*This is popular history as it should be... For this price, buy two and give one to a friend.*"
Terry Cook, a reader from Ottawa, on **Rebel Women**

"*Glasner creates the moment of the explosion itself in graphic detail...she builds detail upon gruesome detail to create a convincingly authentic picture.*"
Peggy McKinnon, *The Sunday Herald*, on **The Halifax Explosion**

"*It was wonderful...I found I could not put it down. I was sorry when it was completed.*"
Dorothy F. from Manitoba on **Marie-Anne Lagimodière**

"*Stories are rich in description, and bristle with a clever, stylish realness.*"
Mark Weber, *Central Alberta Advisor*, on **Ghost Town Stories II**

"*A compelling read. Bertin...has selected only the most intriguing tales, which she narrates with a wealth of detail.*"
Joyce Glasner, *New Brunswick Reader*, on **Strange Events**

"*The resulting book is one readers will want to share with all the women in their lives.*"
Lynn Martel, *Rocky Mountain Outlook*, on **Women Explorers**

AMAZING STORIES

MONTREAL CANADIENS

AMAZING STORIES

MONTREAL CANADIENS

Thrilling Stories from Canada's Famous Hockey Franchise

HOCKEY

by Jim Barber

PUBLISHED BY ALTITUDE PUBLISHING CANADA LTD.
1500 Railway Avenue, Canmore, Alberta T1W 1P6
www.altitudepublishing.com
1-800-957-6888

Copyright 2005 © Jim Barber
All rights reserved
First published 2005

Extreme care has been taken to ensure that all information presented in this book is accurate and up to date. Neither the author nor the publisher can be held responsible for any errors.

Publisher	Stephen Hutchings
Associate Publisher	Kara Turner
Series Editor	Jill Foran
Editor	Joan Dixon
Digital Photo Colouring	Bryan Pezzi

We acknowledge the financial support of the Government of Canada through the Book Publishing Industry Development Program (BPIDP) for our publishing activities.

Altitude GreenTree Program
Altitude Publishing will plant twice as many trees as were used in the manufacturing of this product.

We acknowledge the support of the Canada Council for the Arts which in 2003 invested $21.7 million in writing and publishing throughout Canada.

Canada Council   Conseil des Arts
for the Arts   du Canada

National Library of Canada Cataloguing in Publication Data

Barber, Jim (Jim Christopher Matthew)
   Montreal Canadiens / Jim Barber.

(Amazing stories)
Includes bibliographical references.
ISBN 1-55439-054-0

1. Montreal Canadiens (Hockey team) I. Title. II. Series: Amazing stories (Canmore, Alta.)

GV848.M6B37 2005   796.962'64'0971428   C2005-901369-9

An application for the trademark for Amazing Stories™ has been made and the registered trademark is pending.

Printed and bound in Canada by Friesens
2 4 6 8 9 7 5 3

For fans of the Montreal Canadiens, and those
who just love to hear a good hockey yarn

Contents

Prologue 11
Chapter 1 A Legend is Born: Georges Vezina and
           the Early Days 13
Chapter 2 The Era of the Stratford Streak:
           Howie Morenz 27
Chapter 3 The Punch Line: Glory in the '40s 44
Chapter 4 The Rocket Riot of 1955 58
Chapter 5 Fergie and the Captain: the
           Underrated '60s 72
Chapter 6 A Dynasty in Full Bloom: Guy Lafleur
           and the 1970s 85
Chapter 7 St. Patrick Roy and the Improbable 1993
           Stanley Cup Run 99
Further Reading 115

Prologue

The Montreal Canadiens had been taking a pounding at the hands of the Ottawa Senators all night long.

It was the dark days of winter 1930. With the recent stock market collapse and the Great Depression around the corner, professional hockey provided a great escape from the looming financial and social chaos.

On this night, the Senators were up 4-2 over the Canadiens, one of the elite teams in the league at the time. The Canadiens were hurting, thanks to the absence of their most dynamic and dangerous player — Howie Morenz.

Morenz had made the trip to Ottawa with the team, but an ankle injury was hampering his skating ability, so he was exiled to the bench for the bulk of the game. It was frustrating for both him and his coach, Cecil Hart, the man who had signed him to a professional contract seven years earlier.

With six minutes left in the third period, the defensively strong Senators seemed to have this victory salted away. But Hart heard a familiar voice beckoning him. With a look in his eye that only a coach could understand, Morenz practically begged to be put into the game.

Some say Hart never had a chance to respond. Others say his nod was imperceptible. Whatever the case, Morenz *bounded off the bench and lined up for the face-off.*

As soon as the puck hit the ice, it appeared on Morenz's stick. The Stratford Streak, as he was known, headed straight down the middle of the ice, drawing both defencemen to him. Instead of barging through as he usually did, he deftly passed the puck off to linemate Aurel Joliat, who blasted it home to make the score 4-3.

On his next shift, Morenz found himself with the puck again, skating as if his severe ankle injury was nothing more than a bad itch. He started out with the puck behind his own goal and blew through all Ottawa defenders, some of whom had decided to watch Joliat in case Morenz decided to pass again. This time, Morenz fired a shot so hard into the back of the Ottawa cage that the goalie barely had a chance to blink. Tie game. To make the comeback complete, Morenz scored the game-winning goal in overtime, eliciting cheers even from a normally hostile Ottawa crowd.

The magical Morenz had amazed the hockey world once again.

Chapter 1
A Legend is Born: Georges Vezina and the Early Days

In the spring of 1909, the National Hockey Association had just completed its second season. The Montreal Canadiens, its roster stocked with French-Canadian players, was already one of the top teams in the young league. To generate even more interest among the province's far-flung Francophone populace, the team decided to barnstorm the rest of Quebec.

One of the exhibition games took place in the town of Chicoutimi. The local team was made up of amateur players who were pretty good, but they were not expected to offer much of a challenge to the professionals from the big cosmopolitan city of Montreal. The Canadiens included team stars "Cannonball" Didier Pitre, Eduoard "Newsy" Lalonde,

Montreal Canadiens

and Jack Laviolette. They were expecting a good skate and to practice a few plays while impressing the locals with their prowess. The Canadiens' coach probably suggested taking it easy on the Chicoutimi squad. After all, paying customers never want to see their friends and neighbours humiliated.

One of the Chicoutimi players, goalie Georges Vezina, did not seem concerned about the potential embarrassment about to befall his team. Standing six feet tall, but looking even taller thanks to his lanky frame, Vezina relaxed, leaning against his goalpost.

He seemed almost bored, reported one contemporary hockey commentator, until the overpowering Canadiens began to slice through the fragile Chicoutimi defence. Laviolette, Lalonde, and Pitre all blasted dozens of shots his way, but none past him. Vezina's teammates, who may have been as impressed as the Canadiens with their goalie's prowess, managed to pull together their game long enough to score twice on the bewildered professionals. Quickly exhausted after their improbable outburst, the Chicoutimi players became little more than spectators as the Montreal players stepped up their game and continued to bombard Vezina with shot after shot.

Everyone watching the game fully expected the Canadiens to rally and overcome their deficit to defeat the upstarts. The young goalie seemed unaffected by the whole affair — he was the only person in the building who showed no emotion — as he acrobatically fended off the enemy shots.

A Legend is Born: Georges Vezina and the Early Days

Georges Vezina shut out the mighty Montreal Canadiens 2-0 that night.

Joe Cattarinich, the Montreal goalie who doubled as the team's coach/assistant manager, couldn't help but see the incredible potential in the young netminder. He wanted the "Chicoutimi Cucumber" (so nicknamed for staying cool under pressure) to replace him between the pipes for the Montreal Canadiens. He got his wish at the start of the 1910-11 season.

It was a shrewd move. Vezina and star forward Newsy Lalonde became the defining players of a new era of hockey — the era of the Flying Frenchmen. As the team evolved into the most storied and successful franchise in the history of professional hockey, it must have been hard to believe that the franchise was created as an afterthought — a somewhat vindictive and spiteful afterthought.

The story of the Montreal Canadiens' birth and infancy is wrought with intrigue and conflict. In the wild and woolly era of professional sport in the years preceding World War I, the top professional hockey league in North America was the three-year-old Eastern Canada Hockey Association (ECHA). As well as franchises in Ottawa and Quebec City, the ECHA had three teams in Montreal. One of the three, the Montreal Wanderers, was the best team in the league, winning Stanley Cup championships in 1906, 1907, and 1908.

During the summer of 1909, P.J. Doran, a wealthy businessman and the proprietor of the Jubilee Rink, purchased the team. Rink owners often created or purchased teams to draw people to their buildings, and Doran figured he had made a good deal in obtaining the Wanderers. Since he owned both the rink and the hockey team, he would not have to pay for the privilege of using the building for his hockey team. And he would generate extra revenue from concession and seat sales.

The other ECHA team owners were not happy with this new arrangement, mostly because the Jubilee Rink was a small facility, which meant their cut of the gate would be smaller. The preferred facility in Montreal was the Westmount Arena. Its owners gave the visiting team a higher percentage of the ticket revenue, and threw in extra amenities. The ECHA asked Doran to keep his Wanderers in the Westmount Arena.

Doran thought it a ludicrous request, and refused. Why should he own a team that played in one building, while his perfectly acceptable arena sat idle? The Wanderers' owner dug in his heels.

The other owners wouldn't budge either, but found themselves in a pickle. They couldn't simply toss Doran out of the league. If press and fans got wind that the best team in the league was asked to leave because they couldn't agree on arena arrangements, the danger was poor publicity, or even legal action.

So, in a risky move, the owners of the four other ECHA franchises decided instead to dissolve the league and form a new league — the Canadian Hockey Association (CHA).

A Legend is Born: Georges Vezina and the Early Days

The new league granted franchises to the existing four teams (Ottawa, Quebec City, the Montreal Nationales, and the Montreal Shamrocks) as well as to a new team, the All-Montreals, to be operated by the owners of the Westmount Arena.

The move surprised and infuriated Doran. He was now a man with a team, but no league in which to play. When he applied for a franchise in the new CHA, he was rebuffed.

The new league also made enemies with a young sports-minded businessman, J. Ambrose O'Brien, who had made the trek down from Northern Ontario to apply for membership for the Renfew Creamery Kings (later the Millionaires). O'Brien had been sent to Montreal by his father, Senator M.J. O'Brien, who had made his fortune in the silver and gold mines in northeastern Ontario. There, rival mine owners put together sports teams as a form of entertainment for their workers and their families, as well as for the broader community. Hockey was another mode of competition for these proud men. Substantial wagering on the outcome of the games meant the owners would spend whatever it took to hire the best hockey players. Besides the crown jewel of his personal hockey empire in Renfrew, O'Brien also owned teams in Cobalt and Haileybury.

But Ambrose O'Brien was practically laughed out of the Montreal hotel room. After his meeting with the CHA owners, still stewing from the humiliation, O'Brien found himself seated in the lobby of the hotel when Wanderers manager Jimmy Gardner happened to walk by. Gardner was still smarting, too, at the shabby treatment he and his boss P.J. Doran had received from the CHA. The two men took an instant liking to one another as they commiserated over their mutual misfortune.

The pair began scheming and rented a room in the same hotel where the CHA mavens were prematurely patting each other on the back. Over cigars and cocktails, the two enterprising men would trump their competitors down the hall. They, too, decided to create a league of their own.

They called it the National Hockey Association (forerunner of the National Hockey League). Montreal would serve as the epicentre of the looming war with the rival CHA. The Wanderers would be the anchor franchise of the new league, joined by the O'Brien teams from Cobalt, Haileybury, and Renfrew.

The fathers of the new league decided that they would need five teams, like the CHA. All the other Montreal-based teams, except the CHA's Nationales, were comprised primarily of English players. Gardner threw out the idea of creating an all-French-Canadian team, one that would appeal to the masses of the city. O'Brien believed the team should not simply ice some French-Canadian players, it should embody the flair and artistry of their collective French heritage, and include the very best French-speaking players on the continent.

Tensions between the two language groups in the province of Quebec were always simmering — especially

A Legend is Born: Georges Vezina and the Early Days

in Montreal. Any meeting between an entirely English and an entirely French team could boil over, and the rivalry would certainly draw massive crowds. So the fifth team in the new NHA became Le Club de Hockey Canadien (the Montreal Canadiens).

In the face of this bold move by the rival upstart league, the CHA was undeterred. It was confident that the new league would fall apart as quickly as it came together. What the CHA failed to grasp was that the wealthy O'Briens were prepared to take even greater financial risks for their league.

A bidding war began from the moment the NHA was chartered, on December 2, 1909. Renfrew picked up Fred "Cyclone" Taylor and Frank and Lester Patrick, while the Canadiens went after French-Canadian Newsy Lalonde.

Lalonde had been a star in the sport from the birth of professional hockey: he had played in the Michigan-based International Hockey League in the first few years of the 20th century. Early photos of Lalonde show him boyishly handsome with a somewhat placid expression. Unlike later Montreal stars, like Howie Morenz or Rocket Richard, Lalonde's looks didn't intimidate. But his actions did.

Lalonde was tough: he was not easily bumped off the puck, and he was not afraid to mix it up with any and all comers. "He had a nasty temper and tangled with all the hard-nosed players of his era," confirmed hockey pundit Brian McFarlane. Known as the fastest player of his era, Lalonde was also a deadly goal scorer. "He once scored nine goals in a game, eight goals in a game, six goals in a game (three times) and five goals in a game (six times), and scored 416 career goals in 314 games."

Lalonde was a real student of the game, with remarkable skills of observation. As an 18-year-old playing pro hockey in 1906 with a team from Sault Ste. Marie, he had noticed that the defencemen from the opposing Pittsburgh team would simply loft a long backhanded shot down the ice to end a dangerous offensive foray.

"Once I figured that out," Lalonde said, "I made a point of getting in front of them and then, suddenly, swerving around so that I actually had my back to the defensemen." The very next time the move was attempted by a Pittsburgh player, Lalonde quickly turned around and the puck hit him in the back. He deftly managed to spin around, pick up the disk, and pop it into the goal. He performed the move twice, helping his team win the game 3-1.

The original Flying Frenchman, Lalonde was the biggest prize for the Canadiens, acquired by team assistant manager (and former captain) Jack Laviolette. The concept of the Flying Frenchmen was truly realized with the acquisition of another speedster, the graceful Didier Pitre. Pitre, like Lalonde, was fast and talented, both as a stickhandler and shooter.

Pitre was also tough. Former Ottawa Senators defenceman Cy Denneny remembers how hard it was to check Pitre. "No matter what I did," he told a sportswriter, "Didier would

A Legend is Born: Georges Vezina and the Early Days

get away for a shot on goal." Coach Eddie Gerard suggested that Denneny slash Pitre in the legs, in order to get him angry and off his game. It didn't work; Pitre continued his dangerous and often successful scoring rushes. So, Denneny decided to use a little psychological warfare instead. He began taunting Pitre, repeatedly calling him every name in the book every time he stepped onto the ice. Again, no luck. "A little later, we discovered our mistake," Denneny reported. "Didier didn't fathom a word of English!"

With a solid lineup of players, the Montreal Canadiens Club was doing a booming business both on and off the ice throughout the 1910s. The CHA had ceased to exist before its first season was complete, and the NHA stood alone atop the professional hockey market — at least for a few years.

Although always a competitive and exciting team, Montreal wouldn't make it to its first Stanley Cup final series until 1916. By this time, another rival professional hockey league had been formed on the west coast. Four years earlier, two of the best hockey players in Canada, brothers Lester and Frank Patrick, had convinced their father to help bankroll the Pacific Coast Hockey Association (PCHA). The Patricks, much like the O'Briens a few years earlier, had a stake in each team in the league and began to lure some of the top players from the NHA in order to be competitive. The trustees of the Stanley Cup decided that the Cup would be contested by the respective champions of the PCHA and the NHA.

The team that Montreal faced for the Stanley Cup final

Montreal Canadiens

in 1916 was from the United States. Capitalizing on hockey-mad fans in the American Pacific Northwest, PCHA teams had sprouted in Portland, Oregon, and Seattle, Washington. For its own first final series, the Canadiens hosted the Portland Rosebuds — the first time an American-based team challenged for the Stanley Cup.

The year had been a turnaround one for Montreal. The year before, it had finished — unbelievably — in last place with a 6-14 record. Before then, Montreal had always been a highly competitive team, but the team had suffered through a number of key injuries, including the absence of Lalonde for nearly the entire season.

Although the revitalized Canadiens were expected to win the series, with Pitre, Laviolette, Vezina, and a healthy Lalonde, the westerners shocked the players and the home crowd 2-0 in the first game. They thoroughly out-hustled the Canadiens in every facet of the game.

The Portland Rosebuds were not going to simply let the reputation of the Canadiens' stars defeat them. Fortunately for Canadian hockey honour, Montreal re-asserted itself, winning the next two games in a row. The third contest, a 6-3 thrashing of the Rosebuds, included a dynamic three-goal performance from Pitre. The fourth game was also a real barn-burner, with lots of flashy play, exciting scoring chances, and a 6-5 score in favour of the American team. Late in the fifth and deciding game in Montreal, the Canadiens' unheralded newcomer, Goldie Prodgers, scored to put his

A Legend is Born: Georges Vezina and the Early Days

team up by a goal.

In the final few minutes, Vezina withstood a withering Portland attack to preserve the win. If not for his goaltending heroics, Portland might have been the first American team to win the Stanley Cup. Vezina also solidified his reputation as a money goaltender, playing his best when the rest of his teammates may not have been. His play foreshadowed the performances of future Canadiens netminders Bill Durnan, Jacques Plante, Ken Dryden, and Patrick Roy.

The very next year, spurred on by the spectacular netminding of Vezina and the terrific trio of Newsy Lalonde, Pitre, and "Bad" Joe Hall, Montreal was again in the finals, against another U.S. team, the Seattle Metropolitans. Stocked with former NHA stars, including forward Frank Foyston and goalie Harry "Hap" Holmes, the Metros were known for an offence that was even more potent than that of the Flying Frenchmen. The defending champions opened the series in Seattle with an impressive 8-4 win. Unfortunately, in the next three games, Seattle's offence kicked into high gear. They outscored Montreal (6-1, 4-1, and 9-1) to win the Stanley Cup in four games. Not even the scintillating play of Vezina could prevent a rout in the Stanley Cup finals. So the Canadiens made hockey history again — this time as the opponents for the first U.S.-based Stanley Cup champions.

The Canadiens and the Metropolitans faced off against one another two years later in the Pacific Northwest. It proved to be yet another history-making Stanley Cup final series — not for what happened, but for what didn't happen. In the spring of 1919, World War I had just ended, and tens of thousands of troops were returning to their homes. The incredible relocation and deprivation caused by the war served as a prime breeding ground for a virulent strain of influenza. In scenes reminiscent of the Black Death in medieval Europe, more than 21 million people died all over the world, including at least 50,000 in Canada. And the Pacific Northwest United States was not immune. In the streets of Seattle, many people resorted to wearing masks to cover their faces in the wake of the pandemic. It struck not just the old and infirm, but also the young and healthy — some in the prime of their lives.

"Bad" Joe Hall was definitely in the prime of his hockey career, and had been playing well for the Canadiens throughout the 1919 Stanley Cup series. He had earned the nickname of Bad not because he was a lout of a player, but because he was such a tenacious checker. But in the fifth game, which Montreal ended up winning 4-3, he seemed sluggish and left the game about the halfway mark. The win gave Montreal two victories in the series, matching the two wins of the Metropolitans. The teams had also tied a game, meaning the next game would decide the Stanley Cup.

Too ill to play, Hall was sent to the hospital along with another Canadiens player. After the game, other players started to feel ill, as did the team's owner/manager, George Kennedy. Montreal was not able to ice enough players to fin-

A Legend is Born: Georges Vezina and the Early Days

ish the series. They asked for players from the Victoria club of the PCHA, but Seattle denied the request. Seattle also decided that it would not be sportsmanlike to continue the series against a debilitated opponent. The club could have asked to be awarded the Cup by forfeiture, but did not. So, the series was never finished and no winner for 1919 was ever declared. The Stanley Cup trustees decided that the 1918 winners, Toronto, would retain the Cup. The year 1919 was the only year since Lord Stanley of Preston donated his famous silver bowl that the Stanley Cup was not awarded — until 2004-05. In 2004-05, the NHL season was cancelled by league commissioner Gary Bettman, who cited an intractable labour impasse between the league and the National Hockey League Players Association.

Dying in a Seattle hospital, a victim of the influenza epidemic, Hall never made it back east. Considered one of the better players of his era, he had been a key cog in the Montreal Canadiens hockey machine. With his death, it seemed as though part of the Canadiens died.

While Vezina was still a stalwart between the pipes for Les Canadiens, the Flying Frenchmen grew older and slower. Their results became mediocre. The 1919 finals was the end of an era — but also the beginning of a new one for professional hockey in North America

In that 1919 series for the Stanley Cup, the Montreal Canadiens were no longer representing the NHA. A new league had been created before the start of the 1917-18 season, in a scenario similar to the founding of the NHA in 1909. League owners had decided that the best way to rid themselves of an unruly member of their league was to start another league — this time, the National Hockey League. The Canadiens were one of the founding franchises of the new league, but would not dominate it immediately.

During a game on November 28, 1925, against the Pittsburgh Pirates, tragedy again struck the Canadiens. Their great goaltender — loved by friends, fans, and foes alike — was not himself. Vezina collapsed on the ice during the first period, complaining of weakness and chest pains. Rivers of sweat dripped off him as he was taken to the Canadiens dressing room. Valiantly, he tried to come back onto the ice a couple of times before finally giving up. Even though his team was aware of his fever of 102 degrees that night, most thought he would recover to resume his position between the goalposts. But Vezina was gravely ill. According to reports at the time, he had dropped 35 pounds. The diagnosis was tuberculosis and at that time, TB was almost always fatal. Vezina died in March 1926, the last vestige of the great Montreal teams of the first decade of the Canadiens' history.

However, hope was on the horizon for another golden era with more Flying Frenchmen and one reluctant English-Canadian lad from Stratford, Ontario.

Chapter 2
The Era of the Stratford Streak: Howie Morenz

By 1930, the Boston Bruins had earned a reputation for being one of the toughest teams in the National Hockey League, and they were the defending Stanley Cup champions. They also played in one of the most intimidating stadiums in all of sport, the Boston Garden.

Howie Morenz was not impressed. The speedy forward with the Montreal Canadiens was perhaps the most exciting player in the game since Cyclone Taylor in the 1910s. Morenz's explosive speed, fearless skill, and potent shot made him a bona fide attraction on blades — and an opponent to be reckoned with.

Challenging Morenz on the Boston blueline in this

Montreal Canadiens

mid-season game stood two mammoth sentries charged with protecting the home goal. Together, they had formed the most effective defensive tandem in the league for the past three seasons. Lionel Hitchman was over six feet tall and weighed in at more than 190 pounds. Eddie Shore was about the same size, gifted at skating and making plays, and especially gifted at doling out punishment.

Morenz had been taking a significant amount of physical battering from the Bruins duo all night — but none of it seemed to faze him. Each time he was knocked down, he would get back up, powerful legs churning, and whip down the ice like a water strider on top of a glassy country pond.

The Bruins players felt Morenz was mocking them with his persistence. Yes, they were doing a pretty good job of keeping him off the scoreboard, but he was getting under their skin. Hitchman and Shore decided to take care of the little nuisance once and for all in this game. They would try to sandwich Morenz between them. Surely their combined 400 pounds would be enough to stop the 165-pound Morenz.

The pair developed a tactic where Shore would lunge at Morenz, causing him to bounce over to Hitchman, who would then flatten the forward. Morenz still got up with a grin on his face, and attempted another trademark move on his next rush up the ice. One particular time, its success was pure magic.

Morenz had grabbed the puck and, with piercing eyes,

The Era of the Stratford Streak: Howie Morenz

focused on Cecil "Tiny" Thompson standing at the ready in the Boston goal. Although Hitchman and Shore were still blocking his way, Morenz picked up speed as he raced up the ice. He passed his own players as well as the forechecking Bruins forwards. The classic confrontation was about to begin anew.

Morenz was over the Boston blueline when the two defenders tried to sandwich him again. In the blink of an eye, Morenz gave an extra burst of leg power and smashed into his larger foes. He was slowed down, knocked slightly off balance, but made it through.

Still, Hitchman and Shore figured they had done their job when one of their teammates, who had finally caught up to the play, intercepted Morenz and harassed him enough to prevent him from moving any closer to the Boston goal.

From 25 feet away, Morenz decided to fire a shot on goal anyway. It slammed off the end boards with enough momentum to make it all the way back out to the Boston blueline. Eddie Shore was waiting for it. A legend in the making himself, Shore was considered to be the most offensively gifted defenceman of his era. He could skate as fast as, or faster than, many forwards, and was in full flight by the time he crossed the centre-ice zone, moving in on Montreal netminder George Hainsworth. He seemed to be home free. Everybody but Hainsworth and his two Canadiens defencemen were left in Shore's wake.

Morenz seemed to be helplessly out of the play,

Montreal Canadiens

Howie Morenz

The Era of the Stratford Streak: Howie Morenz

practically as far back in the Boston end as the goalie. "I was watching Howie all the time," said Conn Smythe, future owner of the Toronto Maple Leafs, "and I saw him follow up his shot with a long leap in preparation to circling the net. To this day, I can't figure out how he managed to stay on his skates as he rounded the cage."

But Howie Morenz was chock full of surprises; he was making a career out of exceeding expectations. Legs pumping like the pistons of a steam engine, Morenz weaved his way through the other players on the ice, with no one but Eddie Shore in his sights. As Shore moved towards the Montreal blueline, the puck was suddenly picked off his stick — from in front of him! Morenz had somehow managed to speed past Shore to grab the puck off his stick.

The Stratford Streak didn't simply humiliate Shore by thwarting his scoring opportunity. He pulled away in the opposite direction, and put the puck past Thompson for a goal.

"Shore was absolutely dumbfounded," said Conn Smythe. Smythe was a man noted for both his knowledge of hockey and horseracing, and he knew a thoroughbred when he saw one. "As for me, I actually was unable to move my mouth; I was so awed by the play. Morenz had done what he was to do for years to come — he took my breath away." The incident exemplified the competitive fire of the mercurial Morenz, and solidified his reputation as the most spellbinding player in the game.

Montreal Canadiens

From an early age, Morenz seemed destined to defy the odds. Born in the small Ontario town of Mitchell, but raised in Stratford, Morenz had been only four years old when boiling water badly scalded his legs. In the days before reconstructive plastic surgery, his parents and doctors hoped that the scarring wouldn't keep him from walking. Sports, particularly ones that demanded excessive leg movement like hockey, seemed pretty much out of the question for the youngster.

Even at this tender age, Morenz obviously didn't pay much attention to naysayers. He loved hockey. He ate, slept, and breathed hockey, so he persevered through the pain to play. His obsession may have got his legs working better than if he had stayed more sedentary.

Morenz became an unlikely standout in junior hockey. In 1919-20, as an 18-year-old, he scored 14 goals and added 4 assists in just 5 games. The next season, in 8 games, he notched 19 goals and 12 assists for 31 points and followed that up with a phenomenal 56 points in 13 playoff games.

He became the darling of the whole Stratford hockey scene. During the 1921-22 season, Morenz played 12 games in 11 days for 3 different teams: 4 games with the junior team and 4 with the Stratford Indians Senior Team. He also played for a team from the local Grand Trunk Railroad, later known as the Canadian National Railway (CNR), where he had begun earning his machinist apprenticeship alongside his father.

As a junior, Morenz competed against players aged 16 to 21. As a senior player, he competed against hardened vet-

The Era of the Stratford Streak: Howie Morenz

eran hockey players, ex-pros, or players on their way up to the professional ranks. Like in today's game, a flashy young buck with the potential to embarrass a more senior player was usually singled out for physical attention by the rougher players of the opposing team.

In photographs from that point in his life, the teenaged Morenz didn't look much different than he did later in his career. He was swarthy, his hairline already receding, his face long, his mouth turned upwards in a slight smirk. His eyes were full of steely intensity.

Statistics showed it didn't matter whether he was playing against teens or grown men. In his four junior games that year, Morenz had 17 goals and 6 assists. In the same number of games, in the senior league, he tallied 10 goals and 3 assists. At this time, intermediate and senior level hockey were considered to be nearly on par with the professional game.

Oddly enough, Morenz came to the attention of the Montreal Canadiens brass, not through the Stratford junior or senior teams, but through the railway shop team. The CNR hosted an annual tournament in Montreal for their shops in eastern Canada. In one game, Morenz's Stratford team faced Montreal's Point St. Charles machine shop team at the venerable old Mount Royal Arena. Morenz, as usual, was a standout.

Ernest Sauve, a referee and a former member of Les Canadiens, took note of the slight young man with uncanny hockey skills. After the game, Sauve called his friend Cecil

Montreal Canadiens

Hart, who happened to be the manager of the Montreal Canadiens. Hart, in turn, told his boss, Canadiens owner Leo Dandurand. Dandurand had heard of the young star, and a rumour that the rival Toronto St. Patricks were courting him.

The Montreal Canadiens needed Howie Morenz. The team had not won a Stanley Cup since Georges Vezina nearly single-handedly won them the title back in 1916. Montreal was a solid team, but many of the star players of the team's formative era were either gone or no longer effective. Crowds, even in hockey-mad Montreal, were starting to fade.

The entire National Hockey League was suffering. Before the 1923-24 season, the four NHL teams were all struggling at the box office to one degree or another. Although the Canadiens were surviving, any failure of the Ottawa Senators, Toronto St. Patricks, or Hamilton Tigers would sink the rest of the league, too. Even though each team had a couple of great players, the on-ice product was no longer the entertaining spectacle for the masses that it had been a decade earlier. The play was plodding at times. The games were low-scoring and often lacked great individual plays.

The ticket-buying public had more options now. Jazz clubs and the new phenomenon of motion pictures were drawing crowds. To compete against Laurel and Hardy, Charlie Chaplin, and Rudolph Valentino, hockey had to provide its own dash, glamour, and personality.

Canadiens team-owner Dandurand knew he had to bring in some new blood to shake up his lineup. He also knew

The Era of the Stratford Streak: Howie Morenz

his French-Canadian fan base liked to see artistry on the ice. Making a bold move in 1922, the year before Morenz arrived, he had traded away the talented and beloved Newsy Lalonde. In exchange he landed a skinny young French-Canadian forward by the name of Aurel Joliat.

Weighing barely 135 pounds, Joliat was thrust into a pressure-filled situation. He had to appease the Montreal fans and media who believed it wasn't enough for the Canadiens to win, they had to win with flair. Even in those days, size was an important factor. But Joliat's speed and manoeuvrability could outmatch size any time. Nicknamed "Little Giant" for his courage, he was known for his ability to not merely absorb an opponent's check, but also to spin away from the check before continuing on toward the goal. In his first game as a Canadien, Joliat scored twice, and made several exciting plays. Dandurand, who was at first vilified for trading away the beloved Lalonde, now seemed to be a genius.

At the end of the 1922-23 season, Joliat was entrenched as a fan favourite, but this was not quite enough to put the Canadiens over the top. Dandurand signed free agent Sylvio Mantha, who had impressed the Canadiens manager with his play with a local amateur club. Mantha would be a part of a solid Canadiens blueline for more than a decade, and an integral part of the team's future success. That same season, after great difficulty, considerable expense, and some serious arm-twisting, Dandurand also landed the big fish — a player on whom he banked not only the future of the Montreal Canadiens, but also the future of the National Hockey League.

Howie Morenz — arguably one of the greatest players in the history of the sport — almost didn't play professional hockey. First, Riley Hern, a friend of Dandurand's and former goalie, was sent to Stratford to woo the young man. Thanks, but no thanks, came Morenz's reply. Although armed with a contract worth $2500 for the 1923-24 season, Hern was told by Morenz that he was happy in Stratford, loved playing for his hometown team, and loved his job as a machinist. Leaving kith and kin for the temptations of a cosmopolitan city was viewed as suspect by rural Ontario folk.

Dandurand was about to give up on Morenz when Toronto sportswriter Lou Marsh suggested that Morenz might be better persuaded by cash than a contract. Morenz was apparently never very good at managing his finances. He liked to gamble, buy nice things, and to make loans to anyone down on their luck. He rarely asked for the money back.

Cecil Hart himself made the next trip to Stratford — with an envelope of small bills. He plunked down $850 on the Morenz family's kitchen table so that both Howie and his dad could see that the Canadiens were serious. The money was enough to wipe out a number of Morenz's debts, and even give him a little pocket money. He signed the contract.

Fans in Morenz's hometown, as well as those in Toronto, immediately called Morenz a traitor for agreeing to leave Ontario to play in Quebec. The ink was barely dry on the contract when Morenz, his initial reluctance reinforced

The Era of the Stratford Streak: Howie Morenz

by overwhelming public pressure, decided he had made a mistake.

In the middle of the summer Morenz returned his contract, claiming he couldn't leave Stratford because he was well established there. In a later meeting with Dandurand, Morenz also tearfully admitted that he didn't think he was good enough to play in the NHL. He was afraid that if he failed at hockey, he would have burned his bridges and woud not be able to go back home to work in the railway shop.

The wily Dandurand was too convinced of Morenz's franchise-enriching potential to let him wriggle off the hook. He convinced him to come to the team's fall training camp in Grimsby, Ontario. Dandurand told Morenz that if he tried out camp for two weeks, he could go home if he didn't like it. But he said later he had no intention of keeping this promise and had training staff and veteran players keep tabs on Morenz — in case he tried to sneak away. However, welcomed by the Canadiens players, Morenz performed well enough in practice and exhibition games to convince himself that he could play in the professional league.

In spite of his incredible talent, Morenz was suffering from what might today be diagnosed as an anxiety disorder. He had been reluctant to leave Stratford, not only because he would get homesick, but because he genuinely felt that he wasn't good enough to play in the NHL.

But hockey seemed to fill up his spirit, and give his life purpose and meaning. It's hard to imagine that the homesick, insecure man who almost bailed out on the Canadiens was the same player who caused the entire hockey world to stand up and take notice in the early part of the 1923 season. And it was on his first goal that Morenz's style of play first came to the attention of big-league observers.

He scored on his first shift, on Boxing Day 1923. On defence for the always-tough Ottawa Senators was another rising young star of the league, Francis "King" Clancy. He was a little smaller than Morenz but what he lacked in size he made up for in pluck and tenacity. "I had not seen Morenz play, but everybody in the league had heard plenty about him. To me, the yarns and newspaper stories sounded just too sensational to be true," Clancy told a writer in 1949. "I had also heard that the speedy centre-forward had been making some of the league's veteran defencemen look rather weak, and I resolved that he wasn't going to put anything over on me in front of my hometown fans."

Sizing up Morenz during the pre-game practice, Clancy's opinion of the allegedly formidable Stratford Streak didn't change. "He's just got two skates and one stick, same as I have. He won't get away with trying his fancy stuff on me. I'll pin his ears back the first chance I get," he said. Clancy thought he was ready when Morenz began to bear down on him. He positioned himself directly in front of the streaking Montreal forward, but was ready to make a quick move to the left or right if Morenz decided to deke. He figured he was nicely balanced, that he could move either way, and that he

The Era of the Stratford Streak: Howie Morenz

would nail Morenz.

He figured wrong. "I was flat on my back on the ice. Morenz had skated right up to me and suddenly cut loose with a long snap shot at the net. Then he had followed through at top speed. He hadn't even bothered to try to shift around me. He had merely skated straight into me, and over me!" Clancy recalled.

Clancy went over to the upstart while both players were still in Ottawa's end. He said that he would remove Morenz's head from his shoulders if he tried that move again. Morenz laughed and performed the same move on the next shift.

By giving Clancy a front-row seat for his first goal in the league, Morenz had also given him and the league a taste of what he had to offer. The NHL finally had a bona fide star attraction, like baseball's Babe Ruth. Howie Morenz and the Flying Frenchmen coming to town became a big event. Morenz had not only brought back much-needed excitement, but also the Stanley Cup, to Montreal at the end of the 1923-24 season.

Entrepreneurs in some of the big American cities were building new arenas and looking for attractions like Morenz to fill seats. They brought in Morenz and NHL teams to show fans in their cities what might come their way. After a couple of exhibition games in New York in 1924, a new team — the New York Americans — was created. The NHL also expanded into Boston prior to the start of the 1924 season. The league was back on the rise, a solid business venture, thanks in large part to Howie Morenz and the flash and dash of the Flying Frenchmen.

While the fortunes of the Canadiens ebbed and flowed throughout the 1920s, Morenz's legend kept growing, reaching its pinnacle with back-to-back Stanley Cup wins in 1930 and 1931.

But just as quickly as success came for the Canadiens, it fled. Not skating as fast as he used to, Morenz seemed drained of energy. Goals were sporadic so the Canadiens suffered as a result. By 1934, Morenz was actually booed by some of the Montreal faithful because he wasn't living up to their expectations. The team wasn't winning as often, and Morenz was taking the blame.

Montreal management believed in dealing away a declining asset before it declined too much, like aging superstar Newsy Lalonde. With much consternation and personal anguish, Hart traded Howie Morenz to the Chicago Blackhawks.

Morenz showed his misery on the ice: he scored a paltry eight goals in the Windy City. The removal of the *bleu, blanc et rouge* of Le Club de Hockey Canadien sucked the life out of Morenz. A change of scenery to the Big Apple a year later didn't help matters, even though New York City had been the place where he first leapt to intercontinental fame.

The Canadiens and their fan interest continued to struggle through the mid-1930s. Prior to the start of the 1936-37 season, Hart decided to see if there was any fire left in

The Era of the Stratford Streak: Howie Morenz

Morenz. He reacquired him from the Rangers for cash. While no longer in his prime, Morenz played as if he had been given a blood transfusion and heart transplant. He began to click again with his old linemates, Aurel Joliat and Johnny Gagnon. The Canadiens won more, and the crowds started coming out again.

On the night of January 28, 1937, Morenz was once more the prince who inhabited the hockey castle known as the Forum. As he had done so many times before, dashing down the ice, Morenz broke through the cordon of Chicago Blackhawk defenders at the blue-line. He sped towards the loose puck that had just rattled off the end boards. Defenceman Earl Seibert, outweighing Morenz by nearly 40 pounds, barreled back to his own zone in a desperate attempt to save some face, and perhaps a goal.

"When he came down the ice, he was like the wind," Seibert said, many years later. "There was no way I could catch up with him, but I was able to force him behind the net. Then he tripped and the tip of his skate got caught in the boards, and I hit him. There was no other way of stopping him."

Another account of the incident had the other Boston defender, Andy Blair, playing a more significant role. It suggested that Blair had managed to get in between Morenz and the puck near the end boards. As Howie rounded the net, he deliberately tried to plow through Blair's outstretched stick. But he lost his balance, falling towards the boards. Seibert rounded the net from the other side and crashed into the helpless Morenz, who had hit the end boards with enough force to slice into the wood. The wood held Morenz's skate blade firmly.

With a sickening snap, Morenz's leg — one of the mighty machines that had propelled him to the upper stratosphere of sports stardom — broke in four places. The leg was irreparable, and Morenz, along with most of his fans, friends, and teammates, was inconsolable.

"I cried that night. I knew he wouldn't be back," Aurel Joliat told an interviewer in the early 1970s. "We were very close and I knew that Howie was worried about the fact that he might burn himself out early ... but ... he could only play full out. When his leg shattered that night, I knew there was no way he could come back. He was through and we all knew it."

Depression, drinking, and despondency were the staples of Morenz's diet for more than a month. Occasionally, the gloom would be punctuated by a raucous hospital visit from other hockey players. He drank too much, and soon suffered a nervous breakdown that curtailed his revelry.

His leg healed only enough to support his weight. This time, unlike after the scalding he received as a youngster, there would be no miraculous comeback. The world came crashing down for Morenz and the Canadiens.

On March 8, sick of lying around in a hospital bed all day, Howie Morenz decided he would try to go to the bathroom by himself. He got up out of the bed, put one unsteady foot in front of another, and before he was halfway across the

The Era of the Stratford Streak: Howie Morenz

room, crumpled to the ground. The most plausible explanation of his death is that Morenz tripped and hit his head on the floor. A resulting coronary embolism stopped his heart.

His teammate, Aurel Joliat, had his own version of the cause of Morenz's death. "Howie loved to play hockey more than anyone ever loved anything, and when he realized that he would never play again, he couldn't live with it ... I think Howie died of a broken heart."

Thousands came to centre ice at the Forum to view his casket, which was surrounded by an honour guard of his teammates. Despite his popularity and success, Morenz's spendthrift nature hadn't left his wife and three children much of a financial legacy. The following season, his teammates raised $11,000 by playing a team comprised of NHL all-stars.

When Morenz was laid to rest, so was an era in the history of the Montreal Canadiens. They were still a pretty good team, but began to suffer from the same malaise and fan indifference that they had endured before the Stratford Streak.

Chapter 3
The Punch Line: Glory in the '40s

After the 1939-40 season, the Canadiens almost folded. This was a hard concept to fathom for the longest-running professional hockey organization in the world — and for the hockey hotbed of the nation.

The Montreal Canadiens had finished dead last in the National Hockey League standings, winning only 10 out of 48 games. The team that used to fill the Forum to overflowing 10 years earlier, when Howie Morenz and the Flying Frenchmen were at the top of their game, was drawing a mere 3000 fans. Two years earlier, the other NHL team in Montreal, the primarily English-Canadian Maroons, had folded. Would the Habs be the next casualty?

The other teams in the league decided it would be in

The Punch Line: Glory in the '40s

their best interest to try to keep the team in Montreal and to help the team rebuild. Perhaps the most immediate requirement was someone new behind the Habs' bench. Conn Smythe recommended the Leafs' former coach, Dick Irvin Sr., who had won a Stanley Cup in the team's first season in Maple Leaf Gardens (1931-32). A former star with the old Pacific Coast Hockey Association and the Western Hockey League (WHL), Irvin had begun his coaching career with the Chicago Blackhawks after a serious injury ended his playing career.

Irvin was a tough taskmaster who expected a full-out effort from his players. His encyclopedic mind catalogued each player's strengths, weaknesses, statistics, and tendencies. "Irvin knows his stars so well," wrote former *Toronto Star* sportswriter Milt Dunnell, "he can almost tell them by watching them skate whether they had a second helping of pumpkin pie with whipped cream for dinner a week last Wednesday." Irvin also believed that in order for players to perform at their best, they had to be in great shape. His practices were often long and exhausting.

Irvin also had an eye for talent, but more importantly, he knew how to motivate that talent and put it together for maximum effort and success. The first three years of his job as head coach of the Canadiens was a reconstruction period. The team's loss of their offensive catalyst, Howie Morenz, had been crippling.

One of the heirs apparent, Hector "Toe" Blake, was in

only his second season with the team. But while the team slumped from 1937 until the arrival of Irvin, Blake had persevered as a source of strength and consistency. He was a solid hockey player who had worked his way up through junior hockey in northern Ontario, and senior amateur hockey in Hamilton. After a short stint with the Montreal Maroons, Blake was picked up by the Canadiens towards the end of the 1935-36 season. Known both for his offensive production and defensive responsibility, Blake was no slouch at throwing his body around, or entering into fisticuffs with whomever crossed him. In short, he was a complete hockey player.

A talented scorer and playmaker, Blake won the Art Ross Trophy as the league's top scorer, and the Hart Trophy as the most valuable player in 1939. He was made captain of the Canadiens in 1940.

Coach Irvin liked to relate a story about Blake's vaunted toughness and tenacity. "Toe injured his tailbone one time and was in such pain he couldn't even sit on the bench. Finally our trainer filled a cushion with air for him to perch on. Even then, there was such agony on his face that I was about to send him to the dressing room. Just then, the Leafs tied the score and Blake roared, 'Let me out there!' Before I could answer, he'd jumped over the boards and shot into the action. Moments later, he whistled a pass to Elmer [Lach] and they combined for the winning goal."

Irvin's rebuilding centred on Blake, but sped up considerably with the addition of budding blueline star Kenny

The Punch Line: Glory in the '40s

Reardon and Elmer Lach for the 1940-41 season. A born playmaker and a natural centre, Lach was one of the pluckiest players of his era, fending off numerous injuries that would have felled most other men. Rejected haughtily by the Toronto Maple Leafs, who considered him too small, he had been lured to Montreal after a couple of years of senior hockey in his home province of Saskatchewan.

Lach proved to be a tougher customer than expected. Early in his first season, he decided to get in the face of one of the league's renowned tough guys from Chicago. Earl Seibert was known as the only man with whom Eddie Shore wouldn't tangle. He stood at more than six feet tall and weighed 210 pounds — a brutish giant in those days. Lach was 165 pounds soaking wet, but decided to challenge Seibert one night. As he raced by the Chicago blueliner, he clipped him near the eye. Seibert let the rookie have that one, but warned him about the painful consequences of another such move.

Lach didn't listen, and charged at the bruiser in the next period, hitting him in the eye again. Seibert repeated his threat to Lach. Late in the game, in a mistake made by many rookies before and since, Lach had his head down looking at the puck on the end of his stick. He couldn't see the charging Earl Seibert coming up beside him. He should have been on alert, because three years earlier, Seibert's punishing check had knocked Howie Morenz out of hockey.

The entire Montreal bench held their breath as they watched what was about to befall their young teammate.

Montreal Canadiens

Would history repeat itself? Fortunately, Seibert didn't end the young man's career, he simply slammed into Lach's unprotected midsection and put Lach on the shelf for three months. However, Lach wouldn't let this or other injuries dampen his enthusiasm for the game. His talent and fortitude earned him the respect of his teammates, fans, and even opposing players. Quiet by nature, Lach was probably the least known of the three members of the "Punch Line."

When putting the famous line together, Coach Irvin saw each player as a key cog in the others' success. "They had everything. Courage, competitive fire and tremendous class. They performed like a smooth-running machine. No line was any better. My, but they were tough and talented," he once said.

The competitive fire was epitomized by Maurice "the Rocket" Richard, the third member of the line. He was a sullen but brilliant young player who had dark, brooding eyes and an uncanny ability to score big goals. A renowned talent around Montreal, he had been injured often during his teenage years and was written off as too brittle early in his NHL career.

During the 1943-44 campaign, however, Rocket's body became remarkably durable. He became the most talked about player of the year — exciting and dominating. Before the season began, Irvin figured Lach would be the best centreman for the potent Richard, since Lach was such a great passer and Richard a great finisher. He also decided to put

The Punch Line: Glory in the '40s

the veteran Blake on the line, not only because he could add his own offensive skills, but because he was also defensively responsible, and would keep the other teams honest with his physical presence. Richard thrived on this line.

In the first round of the 1944 Stanley Cup playoffs, Richard, who had finished a respectable 15th in league scoring, was held off the score sheet. Toronto coach Hap Day had sent out Bob Davidson to curtail the Rocket, and he did so in the opening game and then the first period of the second game. Richard's frustration was getting close to the boiling point.

With the black coals of his eyes burning with an intensity no hockey observer had ever seen before, Richard went on a scoring rampage, blowing past Davidson and his mates for three goals in the second period. In the third period, Richard added two more for a 5-1 final. Five goals in one playoff game was a record that would stand for many years. In the finals against Chicago, Richard scored all three goals in a 3-1 win in the second game of the series. For the first and last time in the history of the Forum, the Rocket was named the first, second, *and* third star of the game by sportswriter Elmer Ferguson.

Obviously, Irvin had a budding offensive powerhouse for 1943-44, led by Rocket and the Punch Line. What was still missing at the beginning of the season was a game-saving goalie. It's a well-worn hockey cliché that championship-calibre hockey teams are built from the net out. Irvin had his eye on someone special, but he would have to be patient.

Bill Durnan, a star with a number of junior teams and amateur squads in the Toronto area, had first been on the Maple Leaf organization's radar screen. Besides his confidence and often spectacular puck-stopping ability, Durnan was a rarity for a goaltender. He could hold his goal stick left- or right-handed, depending on which side the opposing forwards were coming in on. He could also catch with either hand. To add to his advantage, Durnan said, "... it often took years before the other guys knew I was ambidextrous."

Horsing around with some friends the summer he was 20, he had seriously injured his leg. Without consulting Durnan or a doctor, the Leafs struck him off their list of players invited to the team's training camp. "When the Leafs found out about my injury they dropped me and I vowed that even when I got better, never would I play pro hockey. I was disillusioned and figured if that was the kind of treatment I was to get, then hell, I didn't want any part of it," he said. Durnan resolved instead to get a good job and make some decent money. Hockey would become his fun sideline. The bad experience kept Durnan out of professional hockey for seven seasons.

He moved to Kirkland Lake and got a job working at one of the mines that dotted the landscape of northeastern Ontario. Beginning in 1936, he also tended goal for the local Senior A club, the Blue Devils. The Kirkland Lake team was good, but no one expected they would be much

The Punch Line: Glory in the '40s

of a challenge to teams from larger centres such as Toronto and Montreal.

With Bill Durnan in goal, however, the Blue Devils made it to the Allan Cup playdowns three seasons in a row, capping off their run by winning it in 1940. At that time, the Allan Cup was held in almost the same esteem in Canada as the Stanley Cup. The conquering heroes, led by Durnan, were feted with banquets, a parade, and other celebrations.

After the Allan Cup win, Durnan took a job in Montreal with the Canadian Car and Foundry Company and played for the Montreal Royals, the top amateur senior team in the city. The team played its home games at the Forum, and was thus under the watchful eye of the Canadiens organization.

Canadiens head coach Irvin and manager Tommy Gorman witnessed Durnan making save after spectacular save for the Royals, while their own team struggled to find a competent netminder. "Big as a horse, nimble as a cat, a real holler-guy and a team sparkplug, Durnan was just what I was looking for," Gorman commented later.

Because of his ill treatment by the Maple Leafs, Durnan was reluctant to sign with the Canadiens. For three agonizing years, the Canadiens management team, the press, and fans hoped Durnan would relent. Mere minutes before the start of the 1943-44 season, Gorman finally got Durnan's name on a contract. Told to rush down to the dressing room immediately, he would start in goal that very evening.

With Durnan between the pipes, the Canadiens now

had the best goaltending to go along with the league's most potent offence. New defenceman Emile "Butch" Bouchard joined an improving defensive corps. Butch was considered to be strong if awkward on the ice, but he had developed a reputation as an unflappable defender, thinking quickly on his feet. He was a key cog in the team's success during the 1943-44 season.

The Canadiens were an improved team, and expectations were high. But in the finals of the Stanley Cup playoffs, the boos rained down from the rafters of the Montreal Forum. There were only 10 minutes left in the third period, and the Canadiens were trailing the Chicago Blackhawks 4-1. Angry at the indifferent, lackadaisical performance of their hometown hockey heroes, Montreal fans wanted to make sure the players knew their feelings.

They were upset, not because the team was in the midst of a losing skid and in danger of being eliminated, but because they might not get to see the Canadiens clinch the Stanley Cup before their eyes. Chicago was a far weaker opponent, and shouldn't have been a real threat to the juggernaut that was the 1943-44 edition of the Montreal Canadiens.

Perhaps the fans could be forgiven for being a little anxious. The last time the Canadiens had been one game away from capturing the most prestigious trophy in hockey was 13 years earlier. In 1930-31, the era of the Stratford Streak, the Canadiens had dominated the NHL. But Howie Morenz was dead, and many of his teammates had retired. Since the

The Punch Line: Glory in the '40s

beginning of World War II and throughout the early 1940s, the Montreal Canadiens had not been living up to the fans' high expectations.

The 13,000 fans jammed into the Forum on April 13, 1944, wanted desperately to re-experience the joy of being on top of the world. They wanted to live vicariously through the players bearing the CH on their chests. And most of all, they wanted the Cup to be awarded on home ice — in front of them that night.

But, with only half a period left in the contest, the Hawks had clamped down, focusing on defence instead of adding to their lead. The Windy City team wasn't stupid. From their manager to their substitute goaltender, they knew the explosive Montreal Canadiens were capable of blasting goals at will. It was time to bar the door in the Forum; the Blackhawks didn't want to take any chances.

Bored with the lack of excitement on the ice and Chicago's stifling play, the chant "fake, fake, fake," began to rumble from the cheap seats. On the ice, the Canadiens players were as frustrated as their fans. With the Punch Line and Durnan, they knew they were the better team, having lost only 5 games in the 50-game season, and none on home ice. They, too, wanted to end the series here so they could celebrate with friends and family.

Athletes get to the top of their sport with a potent combination of talent, determination, and pride. When the Montreal players heard their own fans' jeers, their pride

Montreal Canadiens

kicked in, motivating their determination, which in turn used their latent talent to turn the tide. Long-time Montreal sports journalist Andy O'Brien called it "the most awesome display of sheer hockey fight I have ever seen on a National Hockey League rink." He wasn't exaggerating.

The determined Chicago team was fighting for its pride, too, not to mention its season. No team likes to be swept. If the Blackhawks could steal this game in Montreal, and win the fifth game in front of their always-raucous home fans, who knew what might happen?

The charge off the Montreal bench was led by the Punch Line and the grizzled veteran of the talented trio, Toe Blake. Shortly after the first denigrations descended from the rafters, Blake set up linemate Elmer Lach with a nice pass. Not known for a blistering shot, Lach let one loose about 10 feet from Chicago netminder Mike Karakas. It narrowly missed Karakas' noggin and hit the top corner of the net. The score: 4-2.

Then Lach's linemate made his patented charge in the face of stern Chicago defence. The Rocket backhanded a shot up and over Karakas to make it 4-3, and shifted the mood in the Forum. The jeers had been silenced, and derrieres were inching closer to the end of the hard wooden seats. Nervous looks must have been exchanged between teammates on the Chicago bench. Had they awakened a sleeping giant?

After Rocket's goal, the Punch Line had stayed on the ice. Lach won the next faceoff and passed the puck up to

The Punch Line: Glory in the '40s

Blake. He raced in behind Karakas, fending off slashes, hacks, arms, and legs like an infantryman heading through no-man's-land. He saw Richard moving into position into the slot and hit him with a tape-to-tape pass. Rocket deposited it into the goal with a blinding flick of the wrist.

With the score now tied, the Forum was awash in a sea of overflowing jubilation and nervous expectation. Blake had been in on the first Montreal goal earlier in the game, and was thus sitting on a four-point night. At 9:12 of overtime, after a few desperate rushes by Chicago against Montreal's rookie netminder, Bill Durnan, Blake capped off his effort with the Stanley Cup–winning goal. It was a fitting end.

Cheers replaced jeers as the Canadiens flooded off the ice to celebrate. There was something extra special about this night that might have saved the franchise. Not only had Canadiens fans seen the Cup again after a long wait, they had also seen the ascent of a hockey deity right before their eyes. Proving that his successes in the 1944 playoffs were no fluke, the Rocket went out the following season and scored 50 goals in 50 games, the first time that total had ever been reached in the history of professional hockey.

The 50th goal came in the final game of the regular season, after Richard had been stalled at the 49-goal mark for a couple of games. Against Boston, the Canadiens were up 3-2 and time was running out on the clock. Richard scored his famous goal at 17:45 of the third period — with some assistance from the rest of the Punch Line. "Elmer Lach gave him a hell of a lot of help on that play," the victimized goaltender, Harvey Bennett, told Brian McFarlane. "In fact, Elmer knocked me on my ass and when I was down and out, bang, Richard whipped it in the net."

Over the course of the 1944-45 regular season, the Punch Line had averaged 4.4 points per game. Most games in this era saw four to six goals scored per game — for both teams. The Punch Line also finished 1-2-3 in the scoring race, with Hart Trophy recipient Lach leading the way with 80 points.

Even with the Punch Line and the Hall-of-Fame netminding of Durnan, the Canadiens failed to repeat as Stanley Cup Champions. But the Canadiens were back in contention the following year, and won the Stanley Cup for the second time in three years. The Canadiens were a good team for the remainder of the 1940s, but not the elite team they were at the start of the decade. Irvin's tough methods were starting to wear thin, and by the early 1950s, many journalists and fans thought he was allowing the Rocket's unbridled passions to become an unstable element on the team.

But things weren't a complete disaster. The Montreal Canadiens possessed many fine qualities. The team was still exciting, could still score its fair share of goals, and still had the best goalie in the game plying his trade between the pipes. After winning Vezina Trophies as the top netminder in the NHL six of the seven years he played in the league, Bill Durnan also set a modern-day NHL record. A Chicago

The Punch Line: Glory in the '40s

player scored on him at the 16:15 mark of the third period of a game on February 24, 1949. The next goal he let in was on March 9 — an amazing 309 minutes and 21 seconds of game time later. In the interim, he had four consecutive shutouts, despite 95 shots. Chicago's Gaye Stewart, who finally did get one by, actually apologized to Durnan for breaking his shutout streak. Durnan said, "I had to chuckle over that because, in a way, I was relieved to get it behind me."

But, as had happened in his rookie year, in that fateful fourth playoff game against Chicago, the boos began to cascade down upon Durnan. Already a jumble of nerves, Durnan couldn't take any more, and retired in tears after the Canadiens were knocked out of the 1950 playoffs. "Hockey started to get rough for me at the end of the forties. I began hurting as I was going to be 35 years old in an era when goalies played a whole season without an alternate and there were no such things as masks to protect you," he said.

After a down period in the early 1950s, precipitated by the retirement of Bill Durnan and injuries, Montreal returned to top of the hockey world by winning the Stanley Cup again in 1953. The powerhouse built around the Rocket and several other key building blocks was a dynasty that began under riotous conditions.

Chapter 4
The Rocket Riot of 1955

The game had barely begun in a tense Montreal Forum, yet the hometown's nemesis, the Detroit Red Wings, already had a 2-0 lead over the boys wearing the *bleu, blanc, et rouge*. The usually formidable Canadiens were playing poorly, to say the least. There was a lack of zip in the offence, a lack of focus from the defencemen, and an unusual lack of intensity in goal. Something was bugging this team.

The St. Patrick's Day crowd in 1955 was also showing little of their usual *joie de vivre*. Instead, the venerable old hockey edifice seemed full of another emotion. Patrons gripped their programs tightly in their sweaty palms, barked at the peanut vendors, and reacted more animatedly whenever a hint of an injustice was committed on the ice. Most of

The Rocket Riot of 1955

the 16,000 sets of eyes in the building were not even focused on the game. The Rocket, after all, was not on the ice.

Maurice "the Rocket" Richard was the Canadiens player these fans had paid their hard-earned money to see. The most electrifying man on two blades, he not only represented the fortunes of a hockey team, and the best of the best in the National Hockey League, but also the hopes, fears, and slights of an entire nation of Québécois. This night, so close to the playoff season, he should have been striking fear into the hearts of opposition defenders and tormenting their colleague in goal.

Without the Rocket, the game had become a mere distraction to the crowd at the Forum. The greater drama became the one playing out not far from ice level, in the seats of one of the rows behind the goal judge's booth. Clarence Campbell had sat in those seats for almost every home game since 1946, the year he began his tenure as president of the NHL.

When Campbell made his grand entrance halfway through the first period, an angry rumble had rolled through the building. Spectators — at least those who weren't already blind with rage and still capable of reason — became a little concerned. Most of the other regular attendees couldn't help but take offence at the patrician manner in which he carried himself on this occasion. The dignified Campbell gave them the perception that he considered himself better than most of the French Canadians in the stands.

The mid-1950s equivalent of "You Suck!" emanated

from the peanut gallery around him. "Clarence Campbell, you Anglo *cochon*! Why don't you go back to your rich *Anglais* friends?" To call the Forum a desert-dry powder keg would be a cliché, but not an exaggeration. The fuse had already been lit. Unfortunately for Mr. Campbell, hockey fans, and the city of Montreal, it wasn't a long fuse.

Clarence Campbell was not a man easily intimidated — by any person or by any situation. Not provocative by nature, he was also not one to back down from threats. After all, the Rhodes scholar had been one of the Allied prosecutors during the Nuremberg war crimes trials. He hadn't blinked then. Dealing with a rogue hockey player and conniving team owners were trifling matters compared to Nazi villains Herman Goering and Rudolph Hess.

On March 15, 1955, two days earlier, Campbell had handed down a judgment he thought was fair for the league. Most other hockey observers, at least those outside Montreal, agreed it was not only fair but necessary. The Rocket had been grounded — for the rest of the regular season, and all of the playoffs.

The suspension had shocked the hockey-loving denizens of *La Belle Province*. Their hero, Maurice Richard, had progressed from a promising, if injury-prone, winger to an outright legend, scoring 50 goals in 1944-45. No one in the league had ever done this before. And he accomplished the feat at a time when the teams only played 50 games in the regular season. He won Stanley Cups in 1944, 1946, and 1953.

The Rocket Riot of 1955

Besides an abundance of talent, a quick-release shot, and a powerful skating stride, Richard was blessed with a drive and intensity that made him the most feared goal scorer in the game. The same passion that motivated him to win every battle for the puck, and every duel with an opposition netminder, generated an intolerable level of frustration and rage. For years, everyone inside and outside the NHL knew of Richard's temper.

When he was suspended in 1955, Richard was leading the NHL in overall points, and was on track to win his first-ever league scoring championship. He had two more points than teammate Bernie "Boom Boom" Geoffrion with only two games remaining in the regular season. With the Rocket firing on all cylinders, Boom Boom blasting in goal after goal with the slapshot he invented, and young superstars Jean Beliveau and Dickie Moore doing their share, the Montreal Canadiens had the most formidable attack in the league. They were deadly on the power play. Along with the steady, occasionally risky brilliance of Doug Harvey on defence and the mercurial Jacques Plante making save after spectacular save, the team looked poised to once again win the Stanley Cup in 1955.

As talented as the team was, Richard was definitely the key. "The Rocket was in a class by himself as a hockey player, especially in the playoffs," noted former NHL referee Bill Chadwick to author Brian McFarlane. "He had a nose for the net and from the blue line in, he would explode. If his team

Montreal Canadiens

Maurice "the Rocket" Richard

needed a big goal, the Rocket would get it."

While the Canadiens were putting together the pieces to their championship dynasty in the early 1950s, the Detroit Red Wings were already at the top of their game. From 1948 to 1954, the Wings played in five Stanley Cup final series, winning three: 1950, 1952, and 1954. The team also finished first place in the league standings at the end of the regular season an unprecedented seven times from 1948 to 1955. The roster of future Hall-of-Famers rivalled that of the burgeoning

The Rocket Riot of 1955

Montreal powerhouse. The Red Wings boasted Gordie Howe, Ted Lindsay, Sid Abel, Terry Sawchuk, and Leonard "Red" Kelly. Throughout the early 1950s, they dominated the top of the scoring standings.

With the Rocket as their centrepiece, Montreal began to overtake the Red Wings. But the ascendancy of the Canadiens dynasty was delayed by the events of March 1955. Because while the Rocket may have been the best player in the league, he was also the most volatile. Players on other teams knew just how tightly wound Richard was. If they slashed him, interfered with him, jabbed him with the stick or an elbow, they knew they could make his charcoal-black eyes burn with deeper fury. They might get Richard off his game or removed from the contest with a penalty. Richard had to be disciplined on a number of occasions for losing his cool on the ice. Over the previous few seasons, Richard and Mr. Campbell had come to know one another very well.

In 1947, Richard had been suspended for the third game of the Stanley Cup finals after bludgeoning a couple of Leafs players during the previous game. Using his stick as an offensive weapon seemed instinctive for the Rocket. Often, he was able to channel his anger and frustration through his stick and score a key goal (or five, as in one 1944 playoff game). When pushed past his breaking point, Richard would grab his stick like an axe and attempt to chop the object of his wrath into submission.

The Rocket was not above challenging the authority,

intelligence, and eyesight of officials either. He picked up a number of misconduct penalties each year for excessive bellyaching. One time in 1951, he literally took matters into his own hands with referee Hugh McLean, who was in his first season officiating in the NHL. Richard had taken a slash from a New York Ranger and retaliated in kind. McLean saw only the second slash, and whistled Richard off for two minutes. Richard, eyes alight, frothing at the mouth with rage at the injustice, hounded McLean all over the ice. He earned himself a further 10-minute misconduct to cool off.

The Rocket was known to lie awake all night after a game if he thought he had played poorly, missed a good scoring chance, or been victimized in some way. Still steaming over the incident, Richard confronted McLean the next morning in the lobby of their New York hotel. He went nose to nose with McLean, grabbing the off-duty official by the throat. For the transgression, Campbell fined Richard but did not suspend him.

As these sorts of violent incidents became more common, and as the Canadiens began to dominate the rest of the league, the five other teams clamoured for harsher sanctions against the Canadiens in general, and Richard in particular.

Earlier in the 1954-55 season, in a game that saw Richard score his 401st career NHL goal and get a standing ovation from the crowd at Maple Leaf Gardens, he was checked heavily into the end boards by the Leafs' Bob Bailey.

The Rocket Riot of 1955

Richard, incensed as much for losing a scoring opportunity as for the sharp pain in his lower back, jumped up breathing fire. Richard whacked Bailey with his stick. The weapon was wrenched from his hands by referee Red Storey. Rocket grabbed another stick and went at Bailey again, clubbing him a couple more times before he was restrained. He was disarmed again and sent off to the Montreal dressing room with a game misconduct. Undaunted, Richard returned to the fray — with yet another stick. In their report to the league office, officials claimed that they had to remove four sticks from Richard's possession. Campbell, again showing restraint, only fined Richard $250. The fine enraged the other team managers, particularly Detroit's Jack Adams, whose club would benefit most from a Rocket-less Canadiens team.

A few months later, on March 13, 1955, the Canadiens played in Boston. With four games remaining in the regular season, Montreal was only four points up on Detroit for first place. With much riding on the line, the team was playing a frustratingly lethargic game. They were being outplayed, out-hit, and out-scored by an inferior Boston team. Montreal coach Irvin Sr. laid into his troops during the second intermission, said Geoffrion. Irvin was not adverse to tearing a strip from any player, including the Rocket. Berating them all for their lack of intensity in such an important game, Irvin knew he could get the competitive juices flowing. Richard in particular was susceptible to this type of challenge, and would often take the message to an extreme.

Montreal Canadiens

With Boston leading 4-1, Richard was rushing into the offensive zone when he was checked by defenceman (and former teammate) Hal Laycoe. Geoffrion recalled the episode: "It started with a typical Richard rush. He barreled down the right side with the puck and was preparing for his patented left turn swerve toward the Boston net. As Rocket went around him, Laycoe grabbed him by the waist and held on. Rocket carried him all the way to the corner where Laycoe gave him an elbow to the back of the neck and threw him into the chicken wire at the end of the rink."

Richard, already peeved because of his and his team's poor play, as well as his sore back, blew a gasket. He swung his stick like Mickey Mantle, just missing Laycoe, who retaliated with a home-run swing of his own. His connected, cutting Richard on the scalp and stunning him.

Both benches emptied. Each player found a dance partner wearing the opposing team's jersey. In the midst of the melee, Richard's anger reached fever pitch as he felt the blood stream down his cheek. From the ice, Geoffrion saw what Rocket did next: "He went after the defenceman, breaking his stick across Laycoe's back. At that point, a linesman, Cliff Thompson (who once had been a Boston defenceman) tried to restrain Rocket, but wound up on the ice." Doug Harvey was holding onto another Boston player, but broke free when he saw Thompson get his mitts on Richard. Harvey noticed that while the Rocket was restrained, Laycoe was not, which meant he could still attack a defenceless Richard.

The Rocket Riot of 1955

Harvey pulled Richard and Thompson apart, allowing the Rocket to take a punch. But Richard hit the linesman, not Laycoe. "If I was bleeding from the head like Rocket was and somebody jumped on me like [Thompson did], I would have hit him too," Harvey said after the game, matter-of-factly.

Campbell was not at the game, so he could only go by the reports of the officials. He also had to contend with the vitriol of the other NHL managers, who were questioning Campbell's ability to mete out justice, especially when it came to the league's most volatile player.

With this incident, particularly the attack on Thompson, it seemed that the league had finally had enough of the Richard sideshow. As talented and entertaining as the player was, he was threatening the good name of the league. If Richard was to get only a slap on the wrist every time he went berserk, his type of behaviour could become rife throughout the league and turn away paying customers. An example had to be made of him.

Campbell brought the full weight of his office down on Richard and the Canadiens. He announced the suspension on March 15, lighting the fire that built up to the events on St. Patrick's Day. Newspapers and radio accounts in Montreal fanned the flames of popular discontent. The Rocket was portrayed as just another whipping boy for the Anglos. Campbell was accused of picking on a true-blue Québécois, a regular guy who came from a modest background. According to incensed fans, Richard had had to fight for everything in the face of English domination in the province, and was being targeted simply because he was both talented and French Canadian. Richard and Campbell became the subjects of all the barroom, locker room, and water cooler conversations in the two days preceding the March 17 debacle.

Everyone knew there was going to be some sort of fallout. Campbell's office received threats. He was told he was going to be murdered in a sudden and gruesome manner if he came to the game on St. Patrick's Day. The mayor of Montreal, Jean Drapeau, told the press he also thought there might be trouble at the Forum if Campbell showed up. For the sake of public safety, he urged Campbell to refrain from doing so. The police even offered Campbell bodyguards. But he steadfastly refused to allow the threats to prevent him from doing his job, which included going to the game.

Campbell could not have expected anything more than booing and catcalls from some malcontents that night. Surely a gentleman of his era would not have brought a woman into a bear trap if he thought it was going to snap shut. Campbell's assessment of the situation turned out to be grossly underrated. His companion, Phyllis King, must have been petrified as the first rotten egg came their way, followed by tomatoes, bottles, cups, and programs. Then a man approached Campbell, smiling. Was he coming to show his support for the beleaguered president? The man stuck out his hand, only to close it in a fist and connect with the NHL president's head.

The Rocket Riot of 1955

Seconds later there was a loud bang, followed by billowing mounds of acrid white smoke that filled the building. As soon as the smoke bomb went off, Campbell was whisked away into a room under the seats. Pandemonium ensued in the Forum. Left in the stands were the 16,000 fans, their mood changed from bloodthirstiness to fear. "Is the building on fire?" "Is somebody shooting?" The smoke blinded and choked the screaming and crying people. Fortunately the building was evacuated without serious injury.

By this time, Campbell had already conferred with Forum management and officials from both teams, and had declared the game forfeited to the Bruins. He surmised that it was the Canadiens and their fans who should bear the brunt of responsibility. Why should Boston have to replay a game that they had no role in ending, and that they were already winning? The final result of the game became a secondary consideration to the bedlam that was going on — both inside and outside the Forum.

The exiting crowd joined hordes of people who had gathered in the neighbourhood around the Forum. The fuse that had been lit inside the building had reached its point of detonation and the explosion resounded throughout Montreal's downtown. Rioters smashed windows, looted stores, and damaged cars. Both rioters and police officers were injured in the process.

Blame was cast on all the major parties involved. Campbell was accused of provoking the riot because he had showed up at the game. Canadiens player Geoffrion said Campbell knew things were going to be tense, and he could have stayed away from the Forum until tempers abated. Detroit manager Jack Adams, who loved publicity, blamed the media for the carnage. He told veteran hockey writer Red Fisher, "I blame you fellows, the newspapermen who have built Richard into a hero and idol, a man whose suspension can transform these great hockey fans into a shrieking band of idiots. Now hear this ... Richard is no hero. He let his team down. He let his public down. He let the league down and he let hockey down."

There was also the inevitable politicization of the incident. Noted Canadian author Hugh MacLennan was seated a few rows behind Campbell on the famous night. He believed the Richard riot was a visceral release of decades of French-speaking Québécois frustration. "To understand the feelings of the crowd that night is to understand a good bit of the social conditions of Quebec in the 1950s," he wrote later.

Perhaps the Quiet Revolution, which later spawned the Quebec independence movement, did begin with the Rocket's suspension and riot. But in hockey terms, the riot led to the end of Dick Irvin coaching the Montreal Canadiens. He was accused of encouraging the Rocket's ferocity — to the detriment of the team. Irvin was replaced by one of Richard's former teammates on the famed Punch Line of the 1940s, Toe Blake, whose career had ended after a broken leg. Blake knew the Rocket well and how to handle him. Richard liked

The Rocket Riot of 1955

and respected Blake. It was little coincidence that the violent incidents and disciplinary actions dwindled over Richard's remaining five years in the NHL. At the same time, his team won a record five-straight Stanley Cups from 1956 to 1960. The Rocket also oversaw the introduction of a whole wing of future Hall-of-Famers throughout the 1950s, including his own brother, Henri the "Pocket Rocket" Richard, who would go on to win a record 11 Stanley Cups.

The Richard riot became one more legend in the Habs' colourful history, but it would not be the last of riotous behaviour from their passionate fans.

Chapter 5
Fergie and the Captain: the Underrated '60s

In 1961 — after 11 straight seasons of being in the finals — Montreal was expected to win its sixth straight Cup. Instead, the powerhouse Chicago Blackhawks knocked them off in the semi-finals. The scenario repeated itself over the next couple of seasons, as first the Blackhawks, then the Maple Leafs, playing tough, close-checking hockey, bounced Montreal from the semi-finals.

As the 1963-64 season began, Montreal fans were becoming frustrated. The team that had been in the Stanley Cup finals every year from 1951 to 1960 had not even made it out of the first round of the playoffs. Something was wrong.

Fergie and the Captain: the Underrated '60s

When the Canadiens arrived in an opponent's arena, they weren't generating the same level of anticipation. Nor were visiting teams shaking with fear when they entered the previously formidable Forum.

Missing were the inspirational forces behind much of the Canadiens' success over the preceding decade. Doug Harvey, the best defenceman in the game at the time, had been traded to New York after one season replacing the Rocket as the team's captain. Bernie "Boom Boom" Geoffrion's game had begun to decline, and there was talk that he might retire or be traded. Once the Rocket's red glare faded from the scene, there wasn't quite the same flare, dash, and drama in Canadiens hockey. Toe Blake's coaching abilities were questioned. Manager Frank Selke, nearing the end of his tenure, was no longer seen as the astute assessor of talent he once was. And the current captain, Jean Beliveau, was constantly criticized in the media for his inability to generate the fire and tenacity of the Rocket.

The best junior hockey player of his day, Beliveau's combination of size, speed, and skill has rarely been seen in subsequent generations of hockey. (Mario Lemieux might be the closest in his combination of talent and size.) The darling of hockey fans in Quebec City in the early 1950s, Beliveau played junior hockey with the Citadelles. Then he played semi-amateur hockey for the Quebec City Aces of the Quebec Senior Hockey League, earning nearly as much as Maurice Richard was earning with the Canadiens.

Montreal Canadiens

Beliveau had always stood head and shoulders above his teammates and opponents throughout his hockey career. Certainly, at six feet, three inches tall, he was unusually tall for a hockey player of that era. Filling out at a robust 205 pounds, with one of the longest reaches in the game, he was also blessed with abundant hockey sense, great skating, and an unparalleled vision on the ice. He was also considered to be the premier stickhandler of his day.

As the best player *not* playing for the Montreal Canadiens in the province of Quebec, Beliveau was implored to join the Canadiens from the moment he finished his junior career in Quebec City in 1951. He did try out, playing two regular season games that year, and notching two points. But he remained loyal to the city where he was treated like royalty. He eventually outgrew the league, however, and needed the challenge of playing for the most storied franchise in hockey. Before the start of the 1953-54 regular season — amidst much hoopla and fanfare — Jean Beliveau signed with Les Canadiens. His legend grew exponentially.

Playing on the same team as Elmer Lach, the Rocket, Doug Harvey, and Bernie Geoffrion, Beliveau became an all-star within two years, and won the Hart Trophy as the league's most valuable player in 1956. But as early as 1961, his offensive numbers began to drop off. He averaged only 20 goals per season, down from 38.

When he was voted the team's captain in 1961, he was greatly surprised. Unfortunately the move caused

Fergie and the Captain: the Underrated '60s

dissension in the dressing room. It alienated veteran forward Bernie Geoffrion, who expected to be named captain for his continuing excellence on the ice and his seniority. Beliveau went to manager Frank Selke. He asked to have the captaincy taken away, and instead be given an "A" to wear on his jersey as the assistant captain. Selke told him that it was not in the best interests of the team to go against their wishes. He would not allow Beliveau to step aside.

Beliveau was hampered by two things — injuries that limited his effectiveness on the ice, and the burden of picking up where Richard left off. Considered a failure because he had not led his team to the Stanley Cup, the vigilant Montreal media attacked him on two fronts. Beliveau was called overly sensitive to the criticism that his play was declining, and therefore was not able to lead by example. Or he was too nice, and hadn't developed the killer instincts of the Rocket. "My mental stability was called into question," he recalled in his autobiography. "Was I strong enough to handle all this adversity?" When his desire and passion was doubted, a couple of years of inner turmoil followed.

At the age of 32, prior to the start of the 1963 season, Beliveau went to team owner Hartland Molson to ask whether he should retire. He knew all was not well with the Club and didn't want to be the reason for the team not winning. They needed something Beliveau couldn't give them, he argued.

The Canadiens weren't devoid of top-flight talent. The team still had a number of holdovers from their five-straight

Montreal Canadiens

Stanley Cup winning teams of the late 1950s, including the mercurial Geoffrion, the Rocket's little brother, Henri, newcomer Dick Duff, and the recently acquired Lorne "Gump" Worsley in goal. Youngsters like Gilles Tremblay and Yvan Cournoyer were also on the cusp of stardom, but most of these players were undersized for a league that was starting to value size and toughness.

In the early 1960s, after the retirement of the fiery Maurice Richard, the team was getting pushed around by bigger, more physical teams a little too much for the liking of its management and fans. A talented group, the players were considered too soft and too small for the league. The Chicago Blackhawks, matching Montreal's talent with Bobby Hull, a young Phil Esposito, and goalie Glenn Hall, had larger players and a bruising defensive corps.

Then along came John Ferguson. His reputation had preceded him, so the press already knew he was a bruiser with a decent touch around the net. Fans heard that he had won every fight in the minor leagues, and thrashed some of the toughest men who ever laced up two blades. But the NHL had one of the meanest, Stan Mikita, lining up for the Chicago Blackhawks, not to mention the gritty Toronto Maple Leafs. How was Ferguson going to stand up to the big boys?

"Fergie," as he became known, made his National Hockey League debut for Les Canadiens on October 8, 1963. No one knew for sure what to expect. But it took only 12 seconds for the NHL to view the Montreal Canadiens as a new kind of team.

Fergie and the Captain: the Underrated '60s

Montreal was at home against the Boston Bruins, the team with the self-proclaimed "baddest" man in the game, "Terrible" Ted Green. For the past couple of seasons, Green had run roughshod over the entire league, taking potshots whenever he felt like it against Montreal's finesse players, including team captain Jean Beliveau. Talented as well as mean, he seemed to revel in his role as the Bruins' designated thug.

Lined up for the face-off, Green verbally berated his opposite, occasionally jabbing him with his stick. Ferguson remained calm, almost emotionless. Then, almost as suddenly as the confrontation began, it was over. "Gloves flew off, Ferguson threw a solid right that landed in Green's nostrils. He followed up with a second well-aimed punch and a third furious blow," wrote hockey historian Brian McFarlane. "Green staggered back, shaken by the ferocity of Fergie's attack, his face numb from the punches. He realized there was a new enforcer in the league." He had met his match in John Ferguson.

And the rest of the Montreal Canadiens (including coach Toe Blake, a man who rarely shied away from a scrap in his days as a player) knew they now had that missing piece of the puzzle. The piece that could bring them back to the top of the NHL was physical intimidation.

Ferguson was just one part of the Montreal Canadiens' roster renovation. In the immediate aftermath of Richard's retirement, the team's management had known changes

Montreal Canadiens

were needed. They began deliberately signing players who were known more for their size and grit than their speed and skill. At the same time the Canadiens decided to get Ferguson's name on a contract, they brought in tough-but-mobile defenceman Jacques Laperriere, as well as noted roughnecks Terry Harper and Ted Harris. Former Detroit Red Wing tough guy Bryan "Bugsy" Watson was also signed to add more depth.

The Canadiens were now able to go toe to toe with the Blackhawks and the gritty veteran-laden Toronto Maple Leafs. Gilles Tremblay, an underrated forward for the Canadiens of the 1960s, said he and the rest of the players respected the role players such as Ferguson played on the team. He felt safer playing with them than against them.

"It was necessary to get players like [Ferguson] to let us play our game. On a hockey team with 18 to 20 players, there are role players. Guys like Yvan Cournoyer, Bobby Rousseau and I were there for our speed on wing and ability to get scoring chances. Jean Beliveau, Henri Richard and Ralph Backstrom were there for their ability to set up scoring opportunities and Ted Harris, Jacques Laperriere and Terry Harper kept our defensive zone under control. Fergie, Claude Larose and players like that gave all of the rest of us room to maneuver to do our jobs, while they kept the other team's head up," Tremblay told authors Chrys Goyens and Allan Turowetz.

Ferguson was more than just muscle. He had talent. It was a testimony to his ability as an all-around hockey player

Fergie and the Captain: the Underrated '60s

that he was first put on a line with elegant team captain Jean Beliveau and the scoring phenom Geoffrion. Coach Toe Blake knew that Ferguson had popped 38 goals in his last season in the American Hockey League, and was a pretty good playmaker, having earned 40 assists.

After humbling Ted Green in that October 1963 game (and after serving his fighting major), Ferguson went out and scored an even-strength goal later in the first period. He followed that up with a power-play marker in the second period. Playing on the power play was not something the average enforcer did, but Blake sensed that Ferguson was not the average enforcer. He went with the hot hand. Later in that same period, Fergie also fed a great pass to Geoffrion, who blasted it home for the game's tying goal. One knockout, two goals, and one assist: not a bad debut. "That game was an incredible experience for me, I'll never forget it," Ferguson said many years later.

Fergie made an impression on his teammates in the dressing room, as well as on the ice. "John hated to lose and players on his team were afraid of him a bit. With a guy like him on your team, you don't want to fool around," said Beliveau. "He doesn't have to say anything; all he has to do is look at you, like the Rocket used to."

Fergie's talent might not have been in the same league as the Rocket's, but his desire to win certainly was. Over the second half of the 1960s, Jean Beliveau and John Ferguson were the yin and yang of the new-look Montreal

Montreal Canadiens

Canadiens. The Canadiens still had supremely talented offensive players, such as Beliveau, Henri Richard, and Ralph Backstrom, but they plied their trade as a team in a more workmanlike manner.

Still a work in progress at the end of the 1963-64 season, with injuries slowing them down, the team managed to finish first in the league. In the semi-finals of the Stanley Cup playoffs, they lost to the defending and eventual champions, the Toronto Maple Leafs.

Even with the retirement of a weary Geoffrion at the season's end, the team seemed to be gaining confidence. If not for the new additions, new attitude, and new style of the Canadiens of 1964, the loss of someone as passionate and talented as Boom Boom might have been the final nail in the coffin of the post-Rocket Habs. Instead, the team absorbed the loss and carried on with more determination. John Ferguson took over the emotional leadership in the dressing room.

Throughout the 1964-65 season, the Canadiens played more like a team than a group of superstar players. Players such as Claude Provost and Ralph Backstrom, both known more for their checking ability, came to the fore. No longer the class of the league, offensive dynamos whose reputation for skill and speed preceded them in every NHL building, the Canadiens had to work for their wins, and work they did.

Despite the naysayers, Toe Blake also showed that he could coach a team without the star power of the teams of the 1950s. He knew just what player fit into what role, who had

Fergie and the Captain: the Underrated '60s

the hot hand on a given night. He squeezed the most out of every player on his bench.

He also knew he had the right man wearing the "C" on his jersey, even if many members of the media and fans thought differently. The critics would soon have their comeuppance. Beliveau's leadership skills soared, matching his enormous talent. The fire that seemed to be missing had been rekindled into an inferno.

After the disappointment of 1964, the Canadiens were a team on a mission in the 1965 playoffs. For the first time in a long while, heading into those playoffs, Montreal was considered to be on even terms with their opponents. Underdogs no more, they had a better regular-season record than Chicago. But that fact hadn't meant much for Montreal in the previous three springs.

Chicago still had the firepower of Hull and Mikita up front, while Pierre Pilote was earning his Hall-of-Fame credentials quarterbacking the Chicago power play from his defence position. In goal was one of the most talented and most durable netminders of all time, Glenn Hall.

So, the chore for the Canadiens was not going to be an easy one. Home ice turned out to be a definite advantage, as both teams won each of their first three home games in the series. The Canadiens thus had a chance to clinch the series on home ice.

"When we took to the ice for the final game against Chicago, the Forum fans were Cup-starved, and showed their desire to end our four-year 'drought' with a huge ovation that pumped us from the first drop of the puck," wrote Beliveau in his memoirs.

By the time the first period had ended, the Canadiens were leading 4-0, thanks to goals from Beliveau, Dick Duff, Henri Richard, and Yvan Cournoyer. When the game ended, Jean Beliveau was able to hoist the Stanley Cup over his head for the first time as captain of the Montreal Canadiens. Many who had worried that he didn't have the right stuff to lead the Canadiens were now heaping praise upon his shoulders. He had scored eight goals and eight assists to win the first-ever Conn Smythe Trophy as the most valuable player in the post-season.

Against Detroit the next year, Beliveau scored three goals in the six-game final series to help his team to their second straight Cup. The Canadiens were on a new roll; the word dynasty was mentioned again.

In 1967, Beliveau and young netminder Rogatien Vachon were expected to bring the Stanley Cup back to the Quebec Pavilion for Montreal's Expo 67. "However, somebody forgot to tell Terry Sawchuk, Johnny Bower, and the rest of the Over-The-Hill Gang in Toronto. They sent us down in six games," recalled Beliveau. For hockey fans in Toronto, 1967 had meant a glorious and unexpected run, by a team considered to be too old and inept, straight through the favoured Montreal Canadiens.

After the 1967 playoffs, the NHL expanded from 6 to

Fergie and the Captain: the Underrated '60s

12 teams in such far-flung locales as St. Louis, Pittsburgh, Philadelphia, Los Angeles, Oakland, and Minnesota. The new teams were placed in one division and the older teams in the other. In order to give the new teams a fair shake, the league's brass decided that each division would hold internal playoffs, with the winner of each getting a berth in the Stanley Cup finals.

Montreal made it through to the finals in both 1968 and 1969; their opponent in both years was the St. Louis Blues. The Blues had a strong Montreal component to their success. The team was coached by former Montreal Junior coach Scotty Bowman, and former Canadiens luminaries Jacques Plante, Doug Harvey, and Dickie Moore were on the roster. Montreal still won both series in four-game sweeps.

Hockey buffs often wonder why the Canadiens team of the 1960s gets overlooked despite its achievements. The team, captained by Beliveau and emboldened by the terrifying Ferguson, won Stanley Cups in 1965, 1966, 1968, and 1969. And if not for the incredible netminding of the aged caged wonders, Terry Sawchuk and Johnny Bower, who helped propel Toronto to the Centennial Stanley Cup over Montreal, the Canadiens of the 1960s might have duplicated the five-Cups-in-a-row feat achieved by the celebrated team of the late 1950s.

But, by the late 1960s and into the 1970s, the new amateur draft was affecting the Montreal team's potential. It meant weaker teams had first crack at the top junior-aged talent in the league. Montreal could no longer sign up every talented French-Canadian player, as it had been doing for decades.

Fortunately, the forward-thinking Canadiens organization had an extensive scouting staff and a host of affiliated minor professional and junior teams. Even though they didn't have exclusive rights to all the best young French-Canadian players, they were able to maintain a stable of good prospects, many of whom hailed from Quebec.

Intelligent, well-researched drafting, combined with astute trades and signings laid the foundation for a new dynasty, just as the one led by captain Jean Beliveau was coming to an end with his retirement.

In 1971, the Canadiens used their great depth to make some last-minute trades for the first overall choice in the amateur draft. With it, they were able to secure the talents of the best junior-aged player in the nation. To the delight of Montreal fans, he also happened to be French Canadian. Guy Lafleur donning the uniform of the Montreal Canadiens marked the beginning of a new age of Flying Frenchmen.

Chapter 6
A Dynasty in Full Bloom: Guy Lafleur and the 1970s

Late in the seventh game of the 1979 Stanley Cup playoffs, the three-time defending champions were facing the impossible: elimination on home ice. Playing Boston 13 times in the playoffs over the previous 36 years, the Canadiens had won every single series. The Bruins would have loved to get the huge monkey off their backs, but Montreal was still on a mission. The most dominant team of the late 1970s was in the midst of some pivotal changes both on and off the ice, so they sensed urgency in this fading opportunity. If the Canadiens could win this game, and then defeat the New York Rangers, they could be Stanley Cup champions four years in row. It could be the longest Cup-winning streak since the Rocket-led

Canadiens won five in a row, two decades earlier.

Even though it was only the semi-finals, this series was a classic: the finesse, grandeur, and star power of the Montreal Canadiens facing off against the blue-collar work ethic and bone-crunching physicality of Don Cherry's "Lunch Bucket Brigade." It might as well have been the finals, because awaiting the winner of the series was the New York Rangers. A worthy adversary, the team was nonetheless expected to lose to the winner of the titanic clash between the Bruins and the Habs.

With a little more than three minutes remaining in the tense Montreal Forum, Boston held a 4-3 lead. They were on the verge of knocking off the vaunted Montreal Canadiens and moving on to the finals.

But then the linesman lifted his hand, signaling a penalty. This penalty wasn't for hooking, slashing, or tripping. It was one of the few infractions that came under the purview of the head coach.

"Oh cripes," or something more profane, was probably what Don Cherry said when he realized his error. His team's season, and his job as the head coach of the Boston Bruins, was on the line. "Too many men on the ice" is, of course, the penalty called when the referee does a quick head count and sees more than five skaters from the same team on the ice at the same time. Usually, there's a short grace period when a team is changing lines on the fly, but in this instance, that grace period had been exceeded. The call had to be made.

A Dynasty in Full Bloom: Guy Lafleur and the 1970s

While Cherry was swearing at himself, Guy Lafleur was sitting on the Montreal Canadiens bench, recognizing it was time to go to work. Lafleur was one of those players who had made the transition from being simply a great hockey player to being a legend. In the playoffs, when the season was at stake and an opportunity presented itself, Lafleur was someone who could be counted on to produce. When he saw the Boston player go to the penalty box, he knew instinctively his moment had come.

Cherry also knew this was a make-or-break moment for his team. The Boston Bruins had worked too hard to fold now. Unfortunate as it was to get an embarrassing, and potentially costly, penalty at such a key juncture, the Bruins still led by a goal. They were no slouches at killing penalties. Their goaltender, Gilles Gilbert, had outplayed Ken Dryden for much of the game and had already faced nearly 50 shots on goal. All they had to do was contain Lafleur, and linemates Steve Shutt and Jacques Lemaire, for two minutes and then they could celebrate.

But two minutes against the Montreal Canadiens, on their home ice, was different than killing two minutes against most other teams. Especially when a berth in the Stanley Cup finals was within sight and the opposition was being coached by the master bench tactician, Scotty Bowman.

Bowman had suffered a serious leg injury while playing junior hockey, ending his on-ice aspirations. But the Canadiens had been so impressed with his hockey mind that they kept him around as a coach of some of their junior programs. He progressed through the ranks of the Montreal organization but then jumped ship when the expansion St. Louis Blues were looking for a progressive young hockey coach. He took the team to the Stanley Cup finals in each of their first three years. After a dispute with the St. Louis ownership made him leave the team part way through the 1970-71 season, he returned to the Canadiens' fold.

In Montreal, Bowman demanded complete adherence to his vision of hockey. Each player had a role to play, whether he liked that role or not. But for intuitive players like Lafleur, Bowman could adapt his method to include their idiosyncratic styles. Bowman's genius was a rigid system that required discipline at both ends of the rink, but allowed for flow and improvisation. And he had plenty of creative talent, in addition to Lafleur's, from which to draw.

The Habs' captain when Bowman took over was the "Pocket Rocket." Henri Richard lacked the size and hot temper of his brother Maurice, but was considered to be one of the quickest, most exciting, and dynamic players in the league. He made up for his five-foot-seven-inch frame with an ability to elude checks, score, and set up goals. Of similar stature to Henri Richard, Yvan Cournoyer was even quicker, earning the nickname "Roadrunner" for his elusiveness. With his cherubic face, he was also a fan favourite.

Early in his tenure, Bowman could also look down his bench and see another veteran and future Hall-of-Famer,

A Dynasty in Full Bloom: Guy Lafleur and the 1970s

Frank Mahovlich. Considered to be one of the most naturally gifted players in the history of the game, Mahovlich had an effortless skating stride that complemented his easy-going demeanour. In goal, lanky netminder Ken Dryden was cool under pressure and thrived in the toughest, most important games. On the blueline, veterans such as Jacques Laperriere provided leadership for the crop of young blueliners, including the huge, talented redhead, Larry "Big Bird" Robinson.

Through the retirement of veterans like Henri Richard, players like Frank Mahovlich leaving for the World Hockey Association (WHA), and trades and drafts, Bowman and Sam Pollock continually juggled the supporting cast around the burgeoning stars Lafleur, Dryden, and Robinson. Each season, Bowman worked hard to create the right chemistry. Bowman knew that his great players needed to be great all the time, and that they had to be approached differently than some of the others on the team. As he explained to broadcaster/author Dick Irvin Jr., son of the former Canadiens coach, "I think what you have to do with your top players is you have to make them responsible, make them feel that the team isn't going anywhere unless you guys do it."

Bowman also said there was something special about playing and coaching in Montreal, especially after winning a couple of Cups. The expectations for greatness were unlike what was found surrounding any other sports team. "You knew when the playoffs came, the team was going to give you an ultimate performance. You expected it and I think it spurred them on. Everybody demanded it, there was no place to hide," Bowman said. "What makes the big teams really good is that they get a group of very talented players to forget about the individual accomplishments a great part of the time and play as a team. It's still a team game."

Stars like Guy Lafleur played to win — not just scoring championships, but Stanley Cups. Lafleur was a top player from the moment he laced up his blades in Thurso, Quebec. Throughout his minor hockey days, and his record-setting tenure with the Remparts of the Quebec Major Junior Hockey League (QMJHL), where he won a Memorial Cup, Lafleur's individual skills blended well with the teams he played for. Even as a junior, he preferred scoring goals while winning games.

Because the QMJHL was not considered the equivalent to the junior leagues in Ontario and Western Canada, Lafleur's record-breaking offensive stats were at first perceived as over-inflated. The scoring numbers of other top Quebec players, such as Marcel Dionne and Gilbert Perreault, who had elected to play in Ontario, were given more credence. But Lafleur's junior coach, Marcel Filion, said the criticisms were nonsense. "Lafleur scores so many goals because he works very hard. He never stops. He back-checks, he digs for the puck in the corner, he sets up goals for other players, and he kills penalties when we ask him to do it."

His skating and pure gracefulness on the ice set him apart from his contemporaries. While Gretzky, Howe, and

A Dynasty in Full Bloom: Guy Lafleur and the 1970s

Guy Lafleur

Montreal Canadiens

Richard might have been considered better players in the history of the game, none of them inspired the kind of eloquent, almost poetic, descriptions accorded Guy Lafleur. "He was an amalgam of everything that was good and great about the game — all the more so because his speed, his quickness, his thunderclap of a shot, and his matinee-idol good looks had a deep rooted French flavour to them," penned Red Fisher. The hockey writer also said there wasn't anything more beautiful on a hockey rink than to see Lafleur in full flight: "When he gathered his legs beneath him, deep in his zone for the start of one of his rink-length rushes, he conjured up visions of the first most exciting players in the National Hockey League. When his eye-blinking puck-handling swept him beyond one man and then another, he was Beliveau. When he danced with a spray of ice into the opposition's zone and released his marvelously accurate shot, he was a composite of all of the great shooters who had ever worn the Canadiens sweater. He was all of them, but most of all, he was uniquely Lafleur."

Red Fisher had begun covering the Canadiens the night of the Richard Riot on St. Pat's Day in 1955. So he'd had the chance to see the Rocket and his brother Henri, Jean Beliveau, Doug Harvey, Dickie Moore, "Boom Boom" Geoffrion, and Jacques Plante. But he claimed that no player wearing the Canadiens uniform lifted fans out of their seats more often than Lafleur.

Lafleur was at it again, halfway through the power play, after the Bruins got their too-many-men-on-the-ice penalty.

A Dynasty in Full Bloom: Guy Lafleur and the 1970s

Solid two-way player Jacques Lemaire had picked up the puck from the face-off and carried it over the Boston line. Without having to look back, he dropped a pass behind him. Having played with Lafleur for years, the cerebral Lemaire had no doubt that his linemate had jumped into the offensive zone behind him, and would expect the pass. Lafleur, his blond hair flowing like a lion's mane, did indeed pick up the puck. As he set his sights on Gilles Gilbert, all eyes in the building shifted to the streaking "Flower."

Cherry thought for sure that Lafleur would move in a little closer to Gilbert, try a few dekes to get into a good scoring position. He knew Lafleur had one of the deadliest shots in the league in terms of accuracy, but thought he was on too sharp an angle to Gilbert's left side. "A shot from there would be desperate, but he drew his stick back. He was desperate. For a split second I almost felt reassured. Then his stick swung around the big arc and the blade made contact with the puck ... anything faster than that shot had to break the sound barrier," Cherry wrote in his autobiography. "Almost in the same moment Lafleur slapped the rubber, it bulged the twine in the left side of the net behind Gillie. There went the lead. Boom! Just like that."

The crowd in the Forum went wild. Guy Lafleur and the Montreal Canadiens were back in the game. The score was now tied at 4-4, and the energy was returning to the Montreal bench. A switch had been turned on — like the one in the brain of a shark when it picks up the scent of blood. That

Montreal Canadiens

killer instinct had been forged over the past half dozen years and four Stanley Cup victories.

Sam Pollock had taken over the management of the team in the mid-1960s. Although he had never played the game at any serious level, Pollock was a keen evaluator of talent, an organizational and administrative genius, and a calculating dealmaker. During the 1970-71 season, while Guy Lafleur was tearing up the QMJHL with his 209-point season, Pollock had traded veteran forward Ralph Backstrom to the Los Angeles Kings for some players and draft choices. Earlier, he had dealt for the Oakland Seals' first-round pick, betting that they would end up with the worst record in the overall standings by the end of the season.

Lafleur was going to be the top draft choice, no matter who held the pick, because he was head and shoulders above the rest of the junior-aged stars of the day. Pollock believed Lafleur was destined to wear a Canadiens uniform and was prepared to move heaven and earth to make it happen. Trading Backstrom had meant the Kings would be a better team, and finish ahead of Oakland in the standings. They did, so Oakland's former first pick was used by the Montreal Canadiens to draft Guy Lafleur.

Young Lafleur took a few seasons to get used to life in the big city and the big leagues. By the mid-1970s, the Canadiens had become the best team in the NHL. They were a team built by Pollock primarily through shrewd draft picks like Lafleur. Winning Stanley Cups in 1973, 1976, 1977, and

A Dynasty in Full Bloom: Guy Lafleur and the 1970s

1978, they were the favourites to win it again in 1979.

Before the series began, most pundits were saying Boston would be lucky to win a single game in the best-of-seven series. Some of the Canadiens may have even believed them. Only a tragic line-changing error in the seventh game of the series got them serious about winning.

Cherry admits that the tying goal by Lafleur deflated his team. "I have seen teams in my 11-year coaching career that were down, but none as thoroughly subterranean as this one," he said in his autobiography, *Grapes*. In the intermission before the overtime, Cherry saw downcast faces in the dressing room. Veterans like Brad Park and Jean Ratelle might never get any closer to winning a Stanley Cup. But he knew there was no reason why the Bruins, full of grit and character in the persons of Wayne Cashman, Terry O'Reilly, Stan Jonathan, and Rick Middleton, shouldn't be able to rally. The prize was still in sight: a chance to vie for the Stanley Cup against a lesser opponent.

As hockey fans know, Cherry is never at a loss for words. When he gave his rallying cry in the dressing room, he did his hero, Admiral Horatio Nelson, proud. A fired-up Boston team poured out of the dressing room, ready for battle. Don Marcotte nearly beat Dryden early on, but the Canadiens goalie made a crucial shoulder save. Terry O'Reilly missed the juicy rebound as the puck hopped over his stick. But the Canadiens soon clamped down defensively and turned the tide of action back in their favour.

Montreal Canadiens

In the overtime period, it wasn't one of the future Hall-of-Famers who carried the team, it was the checking line (known today as "the crash and bang line"). Granted, Mario Tremblay and Yvon Lambert were very good players, but not necessarily expected to be game-breakers. Yet, as any coach or manager worth their salt would say, superstars alone do not win championships. Bowman knew that the so-called utility players were the true backbone of a title team.

Lambert and Tremblay had roles to play in Bowman's system. In the overtime of game seven against the Boston Bruins — with all the marbles on the line — they played the unexpected heroes. After a great deal of action in both ends of the rink, Lambert and Tremblay sped up the ice on a rush. The crowd was on its feet, but not expecting Lafleur-like magic.

Nonetheless, Tremblay could dipsy-doodle on the ice with the best of them, and Lambert was a solid two-way player who averaged more than 25 goals per season over his 10-year NHL career. Lambert didn't have the puck as he was crossing the Boston line, but he did have Brad Park covering him. But Lambert managed to elude the usually tough defenceman, just at the time he was approaching the front of the Boston goal. Tremblay was coming up the ice to Gilbert's right with the puck. While the goalie focused on the puck carrier, he trusted that Park would handle Lambert. Lambert was in a perfect position to bank Tremblay's pass in behind Gilbert, who had no chance to slide from one side of the

A Dynasty in Full Bloom: Guy Lafleur and the 1970s

crease to the other to make the save.

In Montreal, all was right with the universe again. The Canadiens had shown their true championship mettle. Once Lafleur began the process, weaving his magic, the New York Rangers proved a mere annoyance. The star-studded Canadiens swept them aside in four straight games.

The team's 22nd Stanley Cup, and their 4th in a row, would be the last for seven years. Bowman had already decided to leave the organization, slighted at not being named the team's general manager when Pollock retired. Ken Dryden and Yvan Cournoyer also retired, while Jacques Lemaire became a playing coach in Switzerland. The injury bug struck Lafleur, Serge Savard, and Guy Lapointe the following season. Pollock's replacement, Irv Grundman, was inept at best. He had a chance to pick future star Denis Savard in the first round of the 1980 draft, but instead picked Doug Wickenheiser. Savard would go on to record 1338 points in 1196 NHL games. Wickenheiser would get 276 points in 556 career NHL games, mostly as a journeyman.

Lafleur retired prematurely in 1985, only to return to the NHL more than three years later with the New York Rangers. The blond hair was thinner, and the brilliant rushes fewer, but he could still perform magic. The first time Lafleur played the Canadiens in the Forum in his comeback season, everyone there, as well as the millions watching from home, felt like they had stepped back 15 years.

The stride, the moves, and even the flowing hair returned

as Lafleur streaked down the right wing, eluding a couple of Montreal defenders. Then he released that patented shot, beating Patrick Roy, and sending the Forum crowd into a state of delirium. If he had also been there that night, Don Cherry might have again muttered something like, "Oh cripes."

Chapter 7
St. Patrick Roy and the Improbable 1993 Stanley Cup Run

For four long hours on June 9, 1993, Montreal was transformed. Instead of a genteel, internationally respected, culturally sophisticated city, it resembled a war zone. Police in riot gear were hopelessly outnumbered by a celebratory throng gone wild. Thousands of people flooded through the brightly lit streets of downtown Montreal, in the mood for mayhem. Hapless motorists were attacked in their vehicles, their door panels pounded, windshields shattered, fenders torn off. The mob smashed hundreds of storefront windows, creating a glassy cacophony of sound that was accompanied by shouts and screams.

At the end of the debacle, 169 people were left injured,

including 49 police officers. Insurance claims totaled more than $2.5 million. More than 100 people were arrested after 92 stores were looted and seriously damaged. Police also investigated at least a half-dozen cases of arson. Charges on the court docket included everything from participating in a riot and concealing stolen goods, all the way up to assaulting a police officer and assault with a deadly weapon. As the pictures were beamed instantaneously by satellite all over the world, Montreal's reputation was once again tarnished.

Imagine what would have happened had the Canadiens *lost* the Stanley Cup!

A few hours earlier, in front of an enthusiastic and appreciative home crowd, team captain Guy Carbonneau had hoisted the most sought-after trophy in the history of professional hockey. He performed the ceremonial lap around the Forum ice surface, giving each section of the crowd a chance to revel in the presence of the Cup. One of the first teammates he handed it to was Patrick Roy. When the transfer happened, the crowd went wild with adulation. The most knowledgeable and hardest-to-please fans in the NHL knew their hockey saviour when they saw him.

Their raucous response indicated Roy's significance in this Stanley Cup win in a way that being named the winner of the Conn Smythe Trophy, as the most valuable player in the post-season, couldn't match. With Roy, the Montreal Canadiens had won their 24th Stanley Cup, ranking them along with the New York Yankees as the most successful

St. Patrick Roy and the Improbable 1993 Stanley Cup Run

sports franchise in the history of professional athletics.

Maybe because the night was warm, or because the victory was so emotionally wrenching, or so unexpected, Montreal residents turned into roaming bands of mayhem-makers. Many of them had not even been at the Forum to witness Roy, Carbonneau, Kirk Muller, Eric Desjardins, John LeClair, and the rest of the players of Le Club de Hockey Canadien carry around the Stanley Cup. Some fans leaving the Forum after the game joined in the revelry, whereas many ran to get out of the maelstrom.

Don Cherry had no trouble at all getting out. The hockey commentator has told the story many times in slightly different ways. When he left the building, rioters apparently took a break from their wanton destruction to wish him well and give him a thumbs up.

The riot must have reminded an older generation of the trouble stirred up in 1955, when Montrealers took to the streets in violent protest, not violent celebration. On that occasion, the riot broke out after the suspension of public hero Rocket Richard. The connection with the Richard Riot didn't end with the scenes of destruction. St. Patrick's Day was the date of that famous event in 1955. In 1993, the stellar netminding of another "St. Patrick" — Patrick Roy — led to the Canadiens' win over Wayne Gretzky and the Los Angeles Kings.

Roy didn't drive out snakes like the original St. Patrick, but he did drive out many shooters. In the playoffs, he backstopped a motley, underdog Canadiens team to a record 10 overtime wins. In order to win the Stanley Cup, a team must win 16 games — four games in four best-of-seven series. The Montreal Canadiens with Patrick Roy won two-thirds of their games in the most gut-wrenching, dramatic fashion possible. It's not called sudden death for nothing. In overtime, there's no second chance for the goaltenders. To win three or four overtime games in a playoff year is pretty remarkable. When a team wins 10, especially consecutively, it's extraordinary. Perhaps there was justification for Roy's saintly nickname, coined by a member of the Montreal media.

To put fans through so much overtime tension must have weakened their sensibilities to the breaking point. When the final buzzer sounded to end the final game of the series, all that pent-up emotion — agony and joy — was let loose upon the streets of Montreal. There had been riots when the Canadiens won the Cup before, in 1986. Roy's mask had yet to be painted in the team colours, and the Habs still had Robinson, Bob Gainey, and Tremblay, their links to the glorious dynasty of the 1970s. But that 1986 celebration paled in comparison to the one in 1993. Some even said 1993's version outclassed 1955's.

For most of the incredible history of the Montreal Canadiens, winning was expected — even demanded. Cup celebrations, especially from the 1950s on, had become routine. When a Cup wasn't paraded through the streets of the city, Montrealers sometimes got upset, but generally didn't

St. Patrick Roy and the Improbable 1993 Stanley Cup Run

take it out on passing motorists. Even when the team lost the Stanley Cup on home ice to the Calgary Flames in 1989, no trouble followed. And that unbelievable loss came after a 115-point regular season and high expectations under coach Pat Burns.

The Montreal Canadiens of 1993 bore little resemblance to the glorious teams that ran roughshod over the NHL in the 1950s and the 1970s. It was a solid, consistent team but lacked the regular superstars in the lineup. This was part of the team's charm in the end. Defence became Montreal's mantra, first under coach (and former star player) Jacques Lemaire, then Jean Perron and Pat Burns, and it hadn't changed much under current bench boss Jacques Demers. Each player had a role to play in the system, from which he wasn't allowed to deviate. If the system was played to perfection, the team won games. But the fans of the Flying Frenchmen weren't used to this sort of lunch-pail hockey.

Instead of Richard, Beliveau, Harvey, and Blake, or Lafleur, Shutt, Robinson, and Dryden, the 1992-93 Montreal Canadiens were led by a gaggle of kids and seemingly washed-up veterans. The kids could barely remember the team's Cup triumph seven years earlier, let alone the dynasty of the 1970s. The vets had only been picked up in the past couple of seasons by an increasingly panicky general manager. The creative swagger and firepower of the former teams was sorely missing from the current team.

The one thing the teams had in common was a legend

between the goalposts. As a fresh-faced rookie in his snow-white mask, Patrick Roy first catapulted the Canadiens — with only a handful of Bowman's old war horses — to a Stanley Cup in 1986. He also won the Conn Smythe Trophy as the top playoff performer. Over the next seven years, the team's on-ice fortunes rose and fell like a boat on rough seas. With his mask eventually painted red, blue, and white, Roy became the anchor in an ever-shifting lineup that saw captains come and go. Fortunately for the fans of the time, they could at least appreciate some of the finest goaltending ever to occur in the Forum.

Roy embodied all the best qualities of Montreal netminders of the past, which contributed to his popularity and success. He was tall, lanky, and cool like Ken Dryden. He was also quirky, arrogant, and often standoffish — even to his own teammates — much like Jacques Plante had been. He could be stingy and spectacular like Bill Durnan, and he projected a winning aura like Georges Vezina. Roy was a winner, and he knew it.

Roy shared the William Jennings Trophy, with fellow Montreal goalie Brian Hayward, for the lowest goals-against average (GAA) in 1987, 1988, and 1989. Roy won it solo in 1992, compiling a 36-22-8 record, a 2.36 GAA, and a save percentage of .914. For Roy, though, 1992-93 was an off year, with a 3.20 GAA and a mediocre .894 save percentage. The team in front of him was considered to be good, but not great enough to win a Stanley Cup. The big story of 1992-93 had not been

St. Patrick Roy and the Improbable 1993 Stanley Cup Run

Patrick Roy

the Habs, but the resurgence of the Toronto Maple Leafs. New general manager Cliff Fletcher had hired Pat Burns away from Montreal over the summer. But once the playoffs began, the most storied franchise in the history of the NHL took over the hockey headlines.

At the end of the regular season, the Canadiens had been third in their division with 48 wins and 102 points. They were two points behind their bitter rivals, the Quebec Nordiques, and seven back of their perennial Stanley Cup rivals, the Boston Bruins. Mario's Pittsburgh Penguins had been the class of the league, winning a whopping 56 games. The man behind the bench for the Pens was the coach who had guided Montreal's 1970s dynasty — Scotty Bowman. With the potent combination of Lemieux leading the Pens on the ice and Bowman in charge behind the bench, Pittsburgh was expected to win its third-straight Stanley Cup.

The Montreal team's first series in the 1993 playoffs proved to be tough, at least in terms of number of games. The Battle of Quebec was rejoined as the Habs and Nords squared off in yet another playoff grudge match. Quebec had been the league's most improved team from the previous season, leaping 52 points in the standings. They boasted one of the most potent attacks in the game in youngsters Mats Sundin (114 points), Joe Sakic (105 points), the gritty Mike Ricci, and Owen Nolan. They also had a diverse and mobile defence corps and solid netminding from veteran Ron Hextall and his understudy, Stephane Fiset.

St. Patrick Roy and the Improbable 1993 Stanley Cup Run

Opposing them was the confident, composed Patrick Roy. The Nordiques did win the opening game of the series 3-2, thanks to an overtime tally by Scott Young. But it would be the last time Patrick Roy would allow a goal in extra time for the remainder of the playoffs.

In the third game of the series, Montreal's Vince Damphousse scored the overtime winner in a 2-1 victory, while another vet, Kirk Muller, scored the winning tally in game five. In that game, Roy took a high shot off his shoulder from the stick of Quebec's Mike Hough. Roy skated off the ice to the Canadiens dressing room with little feeling in his arm. Jaws, hearts, and expectations dropped. A goaltender with only one functioning arm wasn't much good to anyone, even if his name was Patrick Roy.

Roy was replaced by the unfortunate Andre Racicot. His nickname was "Red Light," because of his perceived predilection for allowing goals. In the 1992-93 season, the nickname was unfair, as Racicot compiled a respectable record of 17 wins, 5 losses and a tie. His goal-against average may have been 3.39, but wins were what counted.

After a pair of goals was given up by Racicot in the span of 18 minutes and nine shots, Roy returned to the game, bolstered by a couple of injections to stop the pain. After the game, reporters saw the unique sight of the game-winning netminder, Roy, and the game-winning goal scorer, Muller, both with their arms in slings. Muller had been nursing a shoulder injury for weeks, and had to immobilize his shoulder between games. Both remained in the lineup throughout the remaining three games, including the sixth and deciding game of the series, which an increasingly confident Canadiens team won 6-2. Roy didn't leave his crease again.

In the second round, Montreal met Buffalo. A plucky team, with superstars Pat Lafontaine, Alexander Mogilny, and Dale Hawerchuk up front, and Grant Fuhr and Dominik Hasek in goal, the Sabres took the Canadiens to overtime in three of the four contests. One of the enduring and final images of that series was the future Hall-of-Famer Fuhr, sitting on his behind, looking quite forlorn. Gilbert Dionne had just scored to give the Habs the game and series sweep — in overtime, of course.

Another surprise team, the Islanders, awaited Montreal in the Wales Conference finals. New York had opened up the field when they bumped off the two-time defending champion Pittsburgh Penguins in seven games. After Buffalo, the Islanders had the worst record of any of the playoff teams in the Wales Conference — 87 points. But they were full of energy and enthusiasm to take on Montreal. The team was built on defence by general manager Don Maloney, and coached by Hall-of-Famer Al Arbour. Pierre Turgeon (a future Canadien) was the team's biggest offensive threat, scoring 132 points in the regular season. Steve "Stumpy" Thomas was next with 87. The Islanders hoped to grind the Canadiens into submission. While they certainly caused consternation, they were shunted aside in five games that included two

St. Patrick Roy and the Improbable 1993 Stanley Cup Run

overtimes. Momentum was building, and interest from the rest of Canada was growing too, hoping for a Toronto–Montreal battle for the Stanley Cup.

Roy was ready. In the 1993 playoffs, he didn't win every game, but any he lost were quickly forgotten. And, as befitted Roy's show-stopping demeanour, the team performed this feat in dramatic fashion with more overtime wins in one playoff year than any team in the history of the NHL.

But Roy wasn't alone on the ice. The Canadiens went into the post-season with a group of veterans leading the charge. Some hockey experts believed many of these players had seen better days and that they weren't a good enough team to survive four grueling playoff rounds. Up front, former Maple Leaf and Edmonton Oiler Vince Damphousse was the top offensive performer on the Canadiens roster, notching 97 points. Both Kirk Muller and Brian Bellows played better than critics anticipated. Their calm, veteran savvy proved to be invaluable on an underdog team fighting for respect. For both players, the chance to win a Stanley Cup, after nearly a decade in the league, seemed to be invigorating them.

A number of young players stepped up their game with energetic play and timely goal scoring. Paul DiPietro scored eight goals that post-season, while linemate Gilbert Dionne, Marcel's younger brother by 15 years, had six. John LeClair began to enter into his own as a goal scorer in this playoff series. Rocket Richard was the only other Canadiens player to score game-winning goals, in overtime, in two consecutive matches. LeClair matched that feat.

The man with the "C" on his jersey, long-time Canadien Guy Carbonneau, was the emotional and spiritual leader of the team. A defensive specialist in the Bob Gainey style, he played with more passion and verve. Although he potted key goals, Carbonneau was best known for being a hard-working, two-way player who could check the opposition's best player to a standstill. Carbonneau had been a team stalwart for a decade. He was the link between the newer generation and the old guard of Gainey, Robinson, Lafleur, Tremblay, Savard, and Lemaire. What he had learned from those gentlemen — with their multiple Stanley Cup wins and Hall-of-Fame honours — was what it meant to be a Montreal Canadien. The corollary was what it took to win.

Captain Carbonneau rarely scored more than 20 goals and 55 points per season, but when he spoke up in the dressing room, everyone listened. In 1992-93, injuries had limited him to 61 games, only 4 goals and 13 assists. The merciless Montreal media declared him washed up, and criticized him for the decline in his game. But in the playoffs, Carbonneau began to show the heart of a true champion — the heart of a Montreal Canadiens captain. He scored three key goals and added three assists while playing all 20 Montreal playoff games.

As Montreal knocked off opponent after opponent in the 1992-93 playoffs, the team was beginning to make believers of those who had earlier given them little chance of lasting

St. Patrick Roy and the Improbable 1993 Stanley Cup Run

past the first round. Others were still skeptical, claiming that luck had played as big a role as talent in the team's success thus far. After all, the Canadiens had won seven consecutive games in overtime to that point. Surely their good fortune had to run out some time!

The 100th anniversary of the Stanley Cup finals took place, fittingly, in Montreal, the same city that had produced the first winner in 1893 — the Montreal Amateur Athletic Association (AAAs). In 1993, Los Angeles came in a little weary after their tough and controversial seven-game Campbell Conference championship series against the Toronto Maple Leafs. The hockey world was still abuzz after Wayne Gretzky had accidentally highsticked and cut Leaf superstar Doug Gilmour, without getting penalized. The Great One led the charge as his Kings fought back to win that game, and then the series in Toronto in game seven. Montreal, on the other hand, had been home resting after defeating the Islanders in the Wales Conference final in five games.

But it seemed as though the emotional win had energized the Kings, a team with not only Gretzky, but other experienced Stanley Cup warriors Charlie Huddy, Marty McSorley, and Jari Kurri (all from the Edmonton Oilers dynasty of the late 1980s). The Canadiens might have enjoyed a little too much relaxation and home cooking. On June 1, in front of 18,000 disappointed Forum faithful, even Roy looked lethargic in a 4-1 loss. Wayne Gretzky scored once and added three assists in this first game of the series.

The next night, Carbonneau was at his defensively stifling best. In coach Jacques Demers' office after the first game, Carbonneau had volunteered to be Gretzky's shadow. That meant where Wayne went, Guy would follow. If Wayne double shifted, so would Guy. If Wayne hopped on quickly to take a face-off, Guy would join him in the faceoff circle. Montreal reeled off the first of their consecutive overtime wins, edging the Kings 3-2. Gretzky was practically smothered for the remaining games. Carbonneau did his job by not allowing another great player to do his.

But it may have been Demers himself who played one of the most important roles in the Cup win. Within the cloistered confines of the Canadiens dressing room, scuttlebutt was circulating that Los Angeles winger Marty McSorley was using a stick with an illegal curve on the blade. In his career as an NHL enforcer, McSorley had scored many more knockouts than he had goals. Of all the players on the Kings' roster, he was probably the last one expected to benefit from fooling around with his stick.

Nonetheless, coach Demers trusted the source of this information. In the second game of the series, he had the Canadiens training staff take a closer look during the warm-up before the game. It seemed likely that McSorley's stick was illegal, but no one could be 100 percent certain. A coach with this type of information had to carefully consider its use. If the referee measured the stick upon his request and determined that the angle on the blade contravened the

St. Patrick Roy and the Improbable 1993 Stanley Cup Run

NHL's rules, the offending party would be given a two-minute penalty. But there was a risk, too. If the blade was found to be legal, the complaining team would be given a two-minute minor for "delay of game."

With his team trailing 2-1 in game two, and only 1:45 remaining in regulation time, Demers made his move. He called referee Kerry Fraser over and asked that McSorley's stick be measured. If the stick was legal, Montreal would have to kill a penalty for the rest of the game, which they would most likely lose. They would then have to head back to Los Angeles for the next two games of the series, down two games to none.

The whole season was riding on Fraser's ability to read the stick angle gauge. A tense Forum crowd understood what was happening and the significance of the call. Seated in the Forum stands, fans could only speculate about the curve on Marty's stick. All eyes were on Fraser to make his decision. "It was cut and dried, it really was," Fraser later told broadcaster/author Dick Irvin Jr. "For any player to go into a third period in a Stanley Cup final with an illegal stick was, to my mind, absolutely asinine."

When Fraser signaled for the penalty, Los Angeles coach Barry Melrose — in his trademark mullet — stood in stunned disbelief. So did Gretzky and many of his teammates. But along with the excitement in the stands, a new energy took over the Canadiens bench.

While McSorley was in the penalty box, Montreal defenceman Eric Desjardins scored on a nifty shot, just 32 seconds later, to tie the score at 2-2. An angered and downcast McSorley slunk back to his bench after the goal. Desjardins, well on his way to becoming one of the elite defencemen in the NHL, had great offensive instincts. He had scored the first goal of the game as well, so was within reach of a modern day NHL record. He wasted little time in etching his name in history. Fifty-one seconds into the first overtime period, he scored his third goal of the game. He became the first defenceman to score a hat trick in a Stanley Cup final game.

Montreal would win two more games via overtime before wrapping up the Cup — and starting a riot in the process — after their 4-1 game five win. Perhaps it was Demers' risky decision to call for a stick measurement that turned the emotional tide of the series. But without Patrick Roy, the team might never have made it past the first round. He had led the Canadiens through four tough rounds to the franchise's 24th, and latest, Stanley Cup.

Eleven years have passed since the Montreal Canadiens last held the Stanley Cup. When the team won it so unexpectedly in 1993, it set off a display of excitement unusual for Canada. Destruction aside, it clearly indicated the esteem in which the Canadiens are held by their devoted fans. Despite the longest Stanley Cup drought in the history of the ancient franchise, hope still springs eternal in the heart of every Habs supporter. It is the passion within the heritage of the championship dynasty that has sustained the amazing story of the Montreal Canadiens.

Further Reading

Beliveau, Jean. *Jean Beliveau: My Life in Hockey*. Toronto: McClelland and Stewart, 1994.

Benedict, Michael and D'Arcy Jenish, eds. *Canada on Ice: 50 Years of Great Hockey from the Archives of Macleans*. Toronto: Viking Canada, 1998.

Benedict, Michael, ed. *The Thrill of Victory: Best Sports Stories from the Pages of Macleans*. Toronto: Viking Canada, 2003.

Brehl, Robert, ed. *The Best of Milt Dunnell: Over 40 Years of Great Sportswriting*. Toronto: Doubleday Canada, 1993.

Brown, William. *Doug: The Doug Harvey Story*. Montreal: Vehicule Press, 2002.

Cherry, Don and Stan Fischler. *Grapes: A Vintage Age of Hockey*. Toronto: Prentice Hal, 1983.

Diamond, Dan, ed. *Total Hockey: The Official Encyclopedia of the National Hockey League* (2nd Edition). Kingston, New York: Total Sports Publishing, 2002.

Dryden, Ken. *The Game* (2nd Edition). Toronto: Macmillan Canada, 1993.

Fischler, Stan. *Those Were the Days: The Lore of Hockey by the Legends of the Game*. New York: Dodd, Mead and Company, 1976.

Fischler, Stan and Maurice Richard. *The Flying Frenchmen: Hockey's Greatest Dynasty*. New York: Hawthorn Books, 1971.

Fisher, Red. *Hockey Heroes and Me*. Toronto: McClelland and Stewart, 1994.

Frayne, Trent. *It's Easy. All You Have To Do Is Win*. Toronto: Longmans Canada, 1968.

Geoffrion, Bernard and Stan Fischler. *Boom Boom: The Life and Times of Bernard Geoffrion*. Toronto: McGraw-Hill Ryerson, 1997.

Germain, Georges-Hebert. *Overtime: The Legend of Guy Lafleur*. Toronto: Viking Canada, 1990.

Goyens, Chrys and Allan Turowetz. *Lions in Winter*. Toronto: Penguin Books, 1987.

Further Reading

Holzman, Morey and Joseph Nieforth. *Deceptions and Doublecross: How the NHL Conquered Hockey*. Toronto: The Dundurn Group, 2002.

Hunter, Douglas. *Scotty Bowman: A Life In Hockey*. Toronto: Penguin Books, 1999.

Irvin, Dick. *In The Crease: Goaltenders Look at Life in the NHL*. Toronto: McClelland and Stewart, 1995.

Irvin, Dick. *My 26 Stanley Cups: Memories of a Hockey Life*. Toronto: McClelland and Stewart, 2001.

Irvin, Dick. *Now Back to You Dick: Two Lifetimes in Hockey*. Toronto: McClelland and Stewart, 1988.

MacInnes, Craig, ed. *Remembering Guy Lafleur*. Vancouver: Raincoast Books, 2004.

McFarlane, Brian. *The Habs: Brian McFarlane's Original Six*. Toronto: Stoddart Publishing, 1996.

McFarlane, Brian. *Stanley Cup Fever*. Toronto: Stoddart Publishing, 1992.

McKinley, Michael. *Putting a Roof On Winter*. Vancouver: Greystone Books, 2000.

O'Brien, Andy. *Les Canadiens: The Story of the Montreal Canadiens.* Toronto: McGraw-Hill Ryerson, 1971.

Roche, Bill, ed. *The Hockey Book.* Toronto: McClelland and Stewart, 1953.

Roxborough, Henry. *The Stanley Cup Story.* Toronto: McGraw-Hill Ryerson, 1971.

Ulmer, Michael. *Canadiens Captains.* Toronto: Macmillan Canada, 1996.

Photo Credits

Cover: AP Photo; Imperial Oil – Turofsky/Hockey Hall of Fame: page 62; London Life-Portnoy/Hockey Hall of Fame: page 91; Doug MacLellan/Hockey Hall of Fame: page 105; James Rice/Hockey Hall of Fame: page 30.

Acknowledgments

With this second book for Altitude Publishing, I consider myself fortunate to have now been able to bring to readers the stories of the two most storied hockey franchises in the history of the NHL. As with my first book for the Amazing Stories series, *Toronto Maple Leafs: Stories of Canada's Legendary Team*, picking out only a handful of key events and significant personalities from Les Canadiens' monumental history was a challenge.

Throughout my career, I have had the good fortune to have met and/or interviewed a number of the legends portrayed in this book, including both Maurice and Henri Richard, Jean Beliveau, John Ferguson, Gerry McNeil, Guy Lafleur, and Steve Shutt. All were true gentlemen and wonderful ambassadors, not only for the Montreal Canadiens, but for the sport of hockey. I hope I have told their stories with all of the excitement and drama they have given us over the years.

Thanks must be given to all the great authors and historians who have come before me for compiling a wonderful record from which to do my research. Quotations used in this book came from a number of these sources, including *The Habs: Brian McFarlane's Original Six*, by Brian McFarlane, and *Lions In Winter*, by Chrys Goyens and Allan

Montreal Canadiens

Turowetz. Stan Fischler's *Those Were the Days: The Lore of Hockey by the Legends of the Game*, as well as his books *The Flying Frenchmen*, co-authored with Maurice Richard, and Boom Boom Geoffrion's biography, co-written with the man himself, also provided quotes. Other quotes came from William Brown's fine biography, *Doug: The Doug Harvey Story* and George-Hebert Germain's *Overtime: The Legend of Guy Lafleur*, as well a number of memoirs including Ken Dryden's *The Game*; *Jean Beliveau: My Life in Hockey*; and Red Fisher's *Hockey Heroes and Me*. A number of great quotes also came from Dick Irvin's books, *My 26 Stanley Cups: Memories of a Hockey Life*; *In The Crease: Goaltenders Look at Life in the NHL*; and *Now Back to You, Dick: Two Lifetimes in Hockey*. Last, but certainly not least, Don Cherry's autobiography, *Grapes: A Vintage Age of Hockey*, provided some of the most colourful quotes.

I appreciate the confidence from the Altitude team, especially from Stephen Hutchings and Jill Foran, and the fine, patient editing of Joan Dixon. Finally, I want to thank my understanding wife, Sheri, for allowing me to indulge my hockey passion, and allowing me to turn our den into a repository of endless numbers of hockey books and other related paraphernalia.

About the Author

A veteran of 12 years in the community newspaper business, Jim has won a number of Ontario Community Newspaper Association awards for both layout and writing, as well as a Canadian Community Newspaper Association award for editorial writing.

He most recently captured a sportswriting award from the Suburban Newspapers Association of America, for a story he penned on the 40th anniversary of the death of Tim Horton.

He is currently the Sports, Arts and Lifestyles editor for *The Barrie Advance*, a Metroland community newspaper serving the growing central Ontario city, after stints working for newspapers in his hometown of Newmarket, Port Colborne, Kirkland Lake, Oshawa and Collingwood. Barber has written a book about local hockey heroes from the Collingwood area, as well as *Toronto Maple Leafs: Stories of Canada's Legendary Team*, for the Amazing Stories imprint.

Educated at Trent University in Peterborough, Ontario, and Toronto's Centennial College, he lives in the picturesque village of Nottawa, a few miles from Blue Mountain and the beautiful shores of Georgian Bay, with his wife Sheri, stepsons Robin and David, dog Shadow, and far too many hockey books.

Amazing Author Question and Answer

What was your inspiration for writing about the Montreal Canadiens?

Actually, I was asked to pull a book about the Canadiens together by Altitude. I had already completed *Toronto Maple Leafs: Stories of Canada's Legendary Team*, and I guess they realized I had some knowledge and background in Original Six hockey history and was also used to deadline pressure because of my job in the newspaper business. I was happy to do it, because it's not often you get asked to do something so interesting.

What surprised you most while you were researching the team's history?

Some of the most interesting characters are the lesser-known ones.

What do you most admire about the players featured in this Amazing Story?

For the most part, the athletes portrayed in this book played for the love of the game. The Rocket, at his most successful, made only $25,000 per year. Up until the 1970s, most NHL players had to have summer jobs, so you knew all the blood, sweat, toil, and tears was for more than the money.

Amazing Author Question and Answer

Which Canadiens escapade do you most identify with?

That's a tough one. Scoring all of four goals in my entire seven-year minor hockey career, I can't say that I identify with any of the players or on-ice incidents. But there was this one goal I scored in peewee, where I won the draw, popped the puck between the opposing centre's legs, zipped around him for a clear breakaway on goal (the face-off was at centre ice) and went five-hole for the goal. The very next face-off, I did the same thing, except the goalie made the save. That was the closest I felt to any of the players depicted in this book. It's a stretch, but it's the best I could come up with.

What difficulties did you run into when conducting your research?

Narrowing my search to a few specific incidents and characters. You're dealing with the most storied franchise in the history of hockey in Les Canadiens. The ideas were endless, and it took some tough decisions to pare it down to manageable proportions.

What part of the writing process did you enjoy most?

Talking to the players, or reading first-hand accounts of their lives and on-ice exploits. When you're reading good hockey prose, you can almost smell the stale coffee in the arena.

Why did you become a writer? Who inspired you?

I was encouraged to get into the newspaper business by some friends I had in my early 20s. I learned very quickly that I enjoyed writing about history and hockey. So, writing about hockey history is a perfect fit for me. My high school history teacher, Mr. Ted Ruddy, was a great inspiration. He saw something in me that the other teachers didn't, and encouraged me to read a lot and write a lot.

What is your next project?

I'm working on two more hockey-related books for the Amazing Stories line. One is on the great defencemen of hockey's golden era, and the other is about great goalies from the same pre-1967 expansion golden era. I'm also helping to co-ordinate all future hockey releases under the Amazing Stories banner.

Amazing Author Question and Answer

Who are your Canadian hockey heroes?
Wayne Gretzky, not just for his athletic and now managerial exploits, but because he is also a quality human being.

Jean Beliveau — a true gentleman. He has a regal bearing, with a genuine, human, common touch.

Brian McFarlane. What Pierre Berton is to Canadian cultural and military history, McFarlane is to hockey history. A national treasure.

AMAZING STORIES

by the same author

AMAZING STORIES™

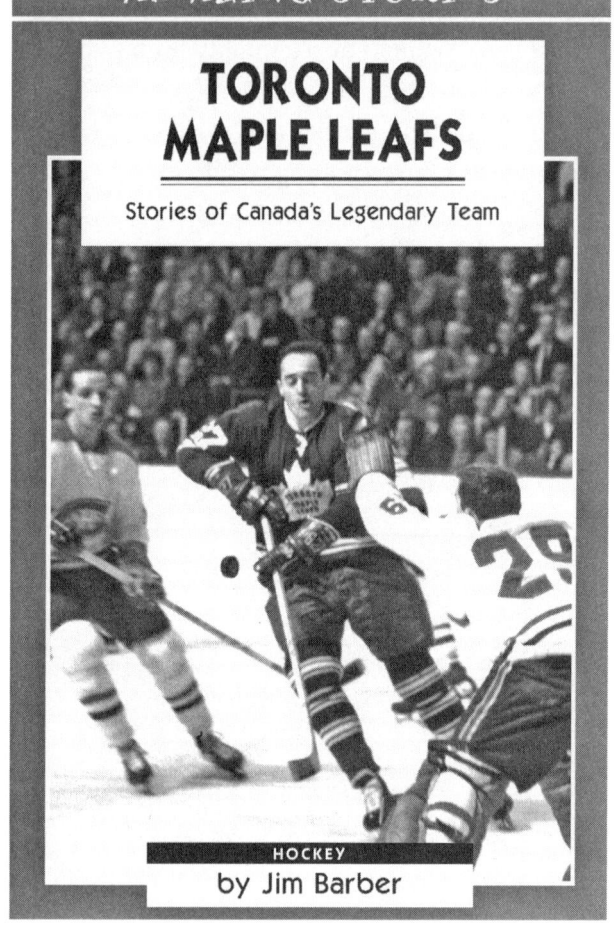

TORONTO MAPLE LEAFS

Stories of Canada's Legendary Team

HOCKEY

by Jim Barber

ISBN 1-55153-788-5

AMAZING STORIES
also available!

AMAZING STORIES™

OTTAWA SENATORS
Great Stories From The NHL's First Dynasty

HOCKEY

by Chris Robinson

ISBN 1-55153-790-7

OTHER AMAZING STORIES

ISBN	Title	ISBN	Title
1-55153-959-4	A War Bride's Story	1-55153-951-9	Ontario Murders
1-55153-794-X	Calgary Flames	1-55153-790-7	Ottawa Senators
1-55153-947-0	Canada's Rumrunners	1-55153-960-8	Ottawa Titans
1-55153-966-7	Canadian Spies	1-55153-945-4	Pierre Elliot Trudeau
1-55153-795-8	D-Day	1-55153-981-0	Rattenbury
1-55153-972-1	David Thompson	1-55153-991-8	Rebel Women
1-55153-982-9	Dinosaur Hunters	1-55153-995-0	Rescue Dogs
1-55153-970-5	Early Voyageurs	1-55153-985-3	Riding on the Wild Side
1-55153-798-2	Edmonton Oilers	1-55153-974-8	Risk Takers and Innovators
1-55153-968-3	Edwin Alonzo Boyd	1-55153-956-X	Robert Service
1-55153-996-9	Emily Carr	1-55153-799-0	Roberta Bondar
1-55153-961-6	Étienne Brûlé	1-55153-997-7	Sam Steele
1-55153-791-5	Extraordinary Accounts of Native Life on the West Coast	1-55153-954-3	Snowmobile Adventures
		1-55153-971-3	Stolen Horses
		1-55153-952-7	Strange Events
1-55153-992-6	Ghost Town Stories II	1-55153-783-4	Strange Events and More
1-55153-984-5	Ghost Town Stories III	1-55153-986-1	Tales from the West Coast
1-55153-993-4	Ghost Town Stories	1-55153-978-0	The Avro Arrow Story
1-55153-973-X	Great Canadian Love Stories	1-55153-943-8	The Black Donnellys
		1-55153-942-X	The Halifax Explosion
1-55153-777-X	Great Cat Stories	1-55153-994-2	The Heart of a Horse
1-55153-946-2	Great Dog Stories	1-55153-944-6	The Life of a Loyalist
1-55153-773-7	Great Military Leaders	1-55153-787-7	The Mad Trapper
1-55153-785-0	Grey Owl	1-55153-789-3	The Mounties
1-55153-958-6	Hudson's Bay Company Adventures	1-55153-948-9	The War of 1812 Against the States
1-55153-969-1	Klondike Joe Boyle	1-55153-788-5	Toronto Maple Leafs
1-55153-980-2	Legendary Show Jumpers	1-55153-976-4	Trailblazing Sports Heroes
1-55153-775-3	Lucy Maud Montgomery		
1-55153-967-5	Marie-Anne Lagimodière	1-55153-977-2	Unsung Heroes of the Royal Canadian Air Force
1-55153-964-0	Marilyn Bell		
1-55153-999-3	Mary Schäffer	1-55153-792-3	Vancouver Canucks
1-55153-953-5	Moe Norman	1-55153-989-6	Vancouver's Old-Time Scoundrels
1-55153-965-9	Native Chiefs and Famous Métis		
		1-55153-990-X	West Coast Adventures
1-55153-962-4	Niagara Daredevils	1-55153-987-X	Wilderness Tales
1-55153-793-1	Norman Bethune	1-55153-873-3	Women Explorers

These titles are available wherever you buy books. If you have trouble finding the book you want, call the Altitude order desk at **1-800-957-6888**, e-mail your request to: orderdesk@altitudepublishing.com or visit our Web site **at www.amazingstories.ca**

New AMAZING STORIES titles are published every month.